More Readers Theatre for Beginning Readers

More Readers Theatre for Beginning Readers

Suzanne I. Barchers and Charla R. Pfeffinger

Readers Theatre

Teacher Ideas Press, an imprint of Libraries Unlimited
Westport, Connecticut • London

Library of Congress Cataloging-in-Publication Data

Barchers, Suzanne I.
   More readers theatre for beginning readers / by Suzanne I. Barchers and Charla R. Pfeffinger.
      p. cm.
   Includes bibliographical references and index.
   ISBN 1-59158-363-2 (pbk : alk. paper)
   1. Children's plays, American. I. Pfeffinger, Charla R. II. Title.
PS3552.A5988M67 2006
812'.54—dc22   2006011825

British Library Cataloguing in Publication Data is available.

Library of Congress Catalog Card Number: 2006011825
ISBN: 1-59158-363-2

First published in 2006

Libraries Unlimited/Teacher Ideas Press, 88 Post Road West, Westport, CT 06881
A Member of the Greenwood Publishing Group, Inc.
www.lu.com

Printed in the United States of America

The paper used in this book complies with the
Permanent Paper Standard issued by the National
Information Standards Organization (Z39.48–1984).

10 9 8 7 6 5 4 3 2 1

For Hunter, Dawson, and Rori, who love a good story.

—S. I. B.

For Cliff, Brad, Heather, and Mickey Daigle, whose smiles and dreams light up the worlds they live and work in.

—C. R. P.

Contents

Introduction ix

Part 1:
Pre-First-Grade Scripts

The Two Frogs 3
The Bear 6
Frank and the Giant 11
The Fish in the Tree and the Hare in the Stream 16
The Little Green Frog 20
Bobino 27
Cat and Mouse, Friends Forever 31

Part 2:
First-Grade Scripts

The Flower Queen's Daughter 39
The Proud Apple Branch 44
The Three Brothers 48
King Frost 53
The Lute Player 57
Clever Maria 61
The Enchanted Prince 66
The Hazelnut Child 70
Blockhead Hans 74

Part 3:
Second-Grade Scripts

The Glass Mountain 81
Big Klaus and Little Klaus 84
Lizzie and the Cats 94
The Monkey Prince 101
The Soldiers and the Dragon 107
Boots and His Brothers 113
Martin and the Magic Ring 118
The Steadfast Tin Soldier 126
The Young Man and His Cat 130

Index 135

Introduction

The Role of Readers Theatre

"Readers theatre is a presentation by two or more participants who read from scripts and interpret a literary work in such a way that the audiences imaginatively sense characterization, setting, and action. Voice and body tension rather than movement are involved, thus eliminating the need for the many practice sessions that timing and action techniques require in the presentation of a play" (Laughlin and Latrobe 1990, 3). Traditionally, the primary focus in readers theatre is on an effective reading of the script rather than on a dramatic, memorized presentation. Generally, there are minimal props and movement on the stage, although with primary students, adding such touches enlivens the production and invites more active participation. The ease of incorporating readers theatre in the language arts program offers teachers an exciting way to build fluency and automaticity into reading instruction.

The scripts in this collection were developed from folktales from a variety of countries, which are noted when known. The readability ranges from 0.5 to 2.8 according to an evaluation using the Flesh-Kincaid readability scale. They are grouped into sections of pre-first-, first-, and second-grade readability levels (parts 1, 2, and 3, respectively). Although readability levels are given, the teacher and students are encouraged to sample all levels of scripts. Each script should be further evaluated by the teacher for features that will assist easy reading: familiarity, repetition, predictability, and so forth. Although children are not expected to memorize the lines in readers theatre, many children will have internalized the lines or a familiar story and will need only the slightest prompting from the script after adequate practice time. Thus, paraphrasing by the reader is common and acceptable. Such success in reading and sharing is highly motivating for the beginning reader. After spending an entire morning exploring and practicing a script, one second-grader asked his teacher why they never had reading that day. She probed for a minute, then gently asked what they were doing as they prepared the script. He lit up in delight, "Oh, we *were* reading!"

Several of the scripts give opportunities for the audience to chime in with lines. This promotes active listening on the part of the students who are listening. Cue cards could be used to prompt the audience. Alternatively, the audience can be instructed as to the lines and to watch a particular narrator for the cue to say the lines. Consider sharing parallel folktales or picture books with similar stories for further experiences in active listening. An additional benefit is the pleasure of performing for parents or other classes and the ease of using a script for special days when a program is expected.

Preparing the Scripts

Once scripts are chosen for reading, make enough copies for each character, plus an extra set or two for your use and a replacement copy. To help readers keep their place, have students use highlighter markers to designate their character's role within the copy. For example, someone reading the role of Narrator 1 could highlight the lines in blue while another student highlights his or her character's lines in yellow. This helps readers track their parts and eases management of the scripts.

Photocopied scripts will last longer if you use a three-hole punch (or copy them on prepunched paper) and place them in inexpensive folders. The folders can be color-coordinated to the internal highlighting for each character's part. The title of the play can be printed on the outside of the folder, and scripts can be stored easily for the next reading. The preparation of the scripts is a good project for a student aide or volunteer parent. The preparation takes a minimum of initial attention and needs to be repeated only when a folder is lost.

Getting Started

For the first experience with a readers theatre script, choose one with many characters to involve more students. Gather the students informally, perhaps in a circle on the floor. Next, introduce the script and explain that readers theatre does not mean memorizing a play and acting it out but rather reading a script aloud with perhaps a few props and actions. Select volunteers to do the initial reading, allowing them an opportunity to review their parts before reading aloud. Discuss how the scripts are alike or different from folktales that the students have heard. Write pronunciations on the board of any challenging words, such as the names of the characters. While these students are preparing to read their script, another group could be reviewing another script or brainstorm ideas for props or staging if desired.

Before reading the first script, decide whether to choose parts after the reading or to introduce additional scripts to involve more students. A readers theatre workshop could be held periodically, with each student belonging to a group that prepares a script for presentation. A readers theatre festival could be planned for a special day when several short scripts are presented consecutively, with brief intermissions between each reading. Consider grouping together related scripts. For example, "Cat and Mouse, Friends Forever" could be paired with "Lizzie and the Cats." Consider these additional groupings drawn from this collection:

Clever Women: "King Frost," "The Lute Player," and "Clever Maria"

Heroes: "The Three Brothers," "The Flower Queen's Daughter"

Persistence: "Blockhead Hans," "Big Klaus and Little Klaus," "The Soldiers and the Dragon"

Once the students have read the scripts and become familiar with the new vocabulary, determine which students will read the various parts. Some parts are considerably more demanding than others, and students should be encouraged to volunteer for roles that will be comfortable for them. Once they are familiar with readers theatre, students should be encouraged to stretch and try a reading that is challenging. Reading scripts is especially useful for remedial reading students, but it is equally important that the students enjoy the literature.

Presentation Suggestions

For readers theatre, readers traditionally stand—or sit on stools, chairs, or the floor—in a formal presentation style. The narrators may stand with the script placed on music stands or lecterns slightly off to one or both sides. The readers may hold their scripts in black or colored folders.

The position of the reader indicates the importance of the role. For example, staging suggestions may indicate that the main characters stand in the center with the other characters flanking them. On occasion, key characters might sit on high stools to elevate them above other characters. The scripts include a few suggestions for positioning readers, but students should be encouraged to create interesting arrangements. For long scripts, chairs or stools help readers from tiring. If students have brief parts or are restless during the script, they could exit the stage after their reading. Students should be encouraged to create fresh ideas for each script.

Props

Readers theatre has no, or few, props, but simple costuming effects, such as royal clothing or flowing gowns, plus a few props on stage will lend interest to the presentation. Suggestions for simple props or costuming are included; however, the students should be encouraged to decide how much or how little to add to their reading. Examining illustrated folktales may give students ideas for enhancements. The use of props or actions may be distracting for beginning readers, however and the emphasis should remain on the reading rather than on an overly complicated presentation.

Delivery Suggestions

Delivery suggestions are not imbedded in the scripts. Therefore, it is important to discuss with the students what will make the scripts come alive as they read. A variety of warm-ups can help students with expression. For example, have the entire class think about how they would react to the following events:

- Discovering school has been canceled because of a snowstorm

- Being grounded for something a sibling or a friend did

- Learning that a best friend is moving

- Getting a new puppy or kitten

- Discovering a sibling ate the last piece of your birthday cake

- Having a genie or fairy appear with three wishes

During their first experiences with presenting a script, students are tempted to keep their heads buried in the script, making sure they don't miss a line. Students should learn the material well enough to look up from the script during the presentation. Students can learn to use onstage focus—to look at each other during the presentation. This is most logical for characters who are interacting with each other. The use of offstage focus—the presenters look directly into the eyes of the audience—is more logical for the narrator of characters who are uninvolved with onstage characters. Alternatively, have students who do not interact with each other focus on a prearranged offstage location, such as the classroom clock, during delivery. Generally the audience should be able to see the readers' facial expressions during the reading. On occasion, it might seem logical for a character to move across the stage, facing the other characters while reading. In this case, the characters should be turned enough so that the audience can see the readers' faces.

Simple actions can also be incorporated into readers theatre. Although primary students are generally less inhibited than older students, encourage presenters to use action by practicing pantomime in groups. If possible, have a mime come in for a presentation and some introductory instruction. Alternatively, introduce mime by having students try the following familiar actions: combing hair, brushing teeth, turning the pages of a book, eating an ice cream cone, making a phone call, falling asleep. Then select and try various activities drawn from the scripts: walking in the woods, meeting a stranger, waving good-bye.

The use of music can enhance the delivery of the play. For scripts with kings and queens, consider preceding the script with a few minutes of music with a royal or stately theme. For example, during "The Two Frogs," a student could beat a simple drum each time the audience says "Hop! Hop! Hop!"

The Audience

When students are part of the audience, they should understand their role. Rehearse good listening practices, plus applauding. Ask students to think about how they would want the audience to react to the reading. Brainstorm things that might go wrong and how to react positively or patiently during the reading.

The Next Step

Once students have enjoyed the reading process involved in preparing and presenting readers theatre, the logical next step is to involve them in the writing process by creating their own scripts. Encourage students to find stories with a lot of conversation as a starting point. Students may want to write the next act in a script—what happens after "happily ever after."

Readers Theatre Online Resources

For more information or scripts, visit www.storycart.com, www.aaronshep.com/rt/, or http://scriptsforschools.com/.

References

Barchers, Suzanne I. *Readers Theatre for Beginning Readers*. Englewood, CO: Teacher Ideas Press, 1993.

Laughlin, Mildren Knight, and Kathy Howard Latrobe. *Readers Theatre for Children: Scripts and Script Development*. Englewood, CO: Teacher Ideas Press, 1990.

Introduction adapted from *Readers Theatre for Beginning Readers* by Suzanne I. Barchers. Englewood, CO: Teacher Ideas Press, 1993.

Part 1

Pre-First-Grade Scripts

The Two Frogs

Summary: Two frogs live near different cities in Japan. They each set out to see the other city. They meet each other along the way and decide to help each other see their destinations. They don't realize that by stretching up their heads, they are each looking back at the town where they began their respective journeys. Compare this story with "The Country Mouse and the City Mouse." Teach the words *Osaka* and *Kyoto* to maintain the beginning readability level.

Readability: 0.5

Staging: Have the narrators stand at opposite ends of the stage. The frogs should start at opposite ends of the stage and walk slowly toward each other once they have begun their journeys. Once they meet and look at their respective homes, they should walk back the other way as the narrators finish the script.

Props: The frogs can dress in green.

Presentation: The frogs can use normal voices. Have one narrator cue the audience in saying *Ribbet! Ribbet!*, and have the other narrator cue the audience in saying *Hop! Hop! Hop.*

Characters:

Narrator One

Narrator Two

Frog One

Frog Two

The Two Frogs

Narrator One: Two frogs lived in Japan. One lived by a lake. It was near Osaka.

Narrator Two: The other frog lived by a stream. It was near Kyoto. Neither frog ever went far from home.

Narrator One: Until this very day.

Frog One: I would like to see the world. I have heard of Kyoto. I think I will go there.

Audience: Ribbet! Ribbet!

Frog Two: I would like to see the world. I have heard of a city called Osaka. I think I will go there.

Narrator Two: Both frogs set out. One walked toward Osaka. The other walked toward Kyoto.

Narrator One: The trip was long.

Frog One: I did not know that Kyoto was so far away.

Audience: Hop! Hop! Hop!

Frog Two: I did not know that Osaka was so far away.

Audience: Hop! Hop! Hop!

Narrator Two: Between the two towns there was a high hill.

Frog One: I did not know that I would have to go up this high hill!

Audience: Hop! Hop! Hop!

Frog Two: I did not know that I would have to go up this high hill!

Audience: Hop! Hop! Hop!

Narrator One: The frogs met at the top of the hill.

Frog One: Ribbet! Where are you going?

Frog Two: Ribbet! I am going to Osaka. Where are you going?

Frog One: I am going to Kyoto. Why are you going?

Frog Two: I want to see the town. Why are you going?

Frog One: I want to see the town. It is a long way.

Frog Two: Yes, it is. What is it like in Osaka?

Frog One: I am not in the town. I live by a lake. There are lily pads and fish. What is it like in Kyoto?

From *More Readers Theatre for Beginning Readers* by Suzanne I. Barchers and Charla R. Pfeffinger. Westport, CT: Libraries Unlimited/Teacher Ideas Press. Copyright © 2006.

Frog Two: I am not in the town. I live by a stream. There are reeds and fish.

Frog One: It sounds like my home.

Frog Two: It is too bad we are not taller. We could see the towns from here.

Frog One: We could stand on our hind legs.

Frog Two: We could hold on to each other.

Frog One: Then we could see.

Frog Two: Let's do it!

Narrator One: The frogs stood as tall as they could. They leaned on each other. They lifted their heads up high. They looked and looked.

Narrator Two: The frogs forgot that their eyes were at the backs of their heads. When they stood up so high, their eyes were looking back the other way. The frog from Osaka was looking at Osaka.

Narrator One: The frog from Kyoto was looking at Kyoto.

Frog One: Oh no! Kyoto looks just like Osaka!

Frog Two: On no! Osaka looks just like Kyoto!

Frog One: Kyoto is not worth the long walk.

Frog Two: Osaka is not worth the long walk!

Frog One: I think I will go back home. I am glad we met.

Frog Two: And I think I will go back home. I am glad we met.

Narrator One: The frog from Osaka hopped home.

Audience: Hop! Hop! Hop!

Narrator One: The frog from Kyoto hopped home.

Audience: Hop! Hop! Hop!

Narrator One and Narrator Two: They lived happily ever after.

From *More Readers Theatre for Beginning Readers* by Suzanne I. Barchers and Charla R. Pfeffinger.
Westport, CT: Libraries Unlimited/Teacher Ideas Press. Copyright © 2006.

The Bear

Summary: In this story of unknown origin, a young princess, June, escapes a domineering father with the help of a nurse who advises her to obtain a bearskin and a cart from the king. The nurse gives her a magic wand, and June escapes the kingdom, disguised as a bear. She meets a prince who takes her home, thinking she's a talking bear. Similar to Cinderella, June goes to a series of balls in beautiful gowns, where the prince falls in love with her. Eventually she reveals her true self.

Readability: 0.5

Staging: The narrators can stand to one side, with the nurse and the king next to them. The nurse and king can leave the stage after their parts. June can sit on a tall stool in the center. The prince can sit next to June, and the queen can sit next to him on a chair.

Props: Consider adding a cart, bearskin, or stuffed bear and a mural portraying woods.

Presentation: The prince can turn slightly as he talks to June and to the queen. Simple costumes appropriate to the roles can be added.

Characters:

Narrator One

Narrator Two

June

Nurse

King

Prince

Queen

The Bear

Narrator One: Once there was a king. He was so proud of his daughter, June.

Narrator Two: He loved her so much. He was afraid she might be hurt. So he would not let her leave the palace.

Narrator One: June did not like this at all. She spoke with her nurse.

June: I am sick of staying in the palace. I want to take a long walk. I want to see things. I want to go places.

Nurse: Hush, June. You know the king wants to keep you safe.

June: I know. But I don't care. I want to feel the rain and see the sun.

Nurse: Stop that kind of talk. The king would give you the stars in the sky.

June: He can't. But he could let me feel the sun on my face.

Nurse: Hush, June. Try not to be sad.

Narrator Two: But June was sad. She longed to go for a walk. She would not stop begging her nurse to let her go.

Nurse: Look. The king will not let you go out of the palace. But I have an idea. Ask him for a cart made of wood. And ask him for a bearskin.

June: How will that help?

Nurse: Just trust me.

Narrator One: June did as her nurse asked. She went to see the king.

June: Father, I would like a cart made of wood.

King: That sounds like it could be fun for you. I'll have one made.

June: And I want a bearskin.

King: Why?

June: It's just for fun. May I have one?

King: I don't see why you need a bearskin.

June: Please, Father. You never let me leave the house. Do this for me. I just want to have some fun.

King: All right. It is hard to say no to you.

June: Thank you, Father.

Narrator Two: A few days later, June had her cart and bearskin. She showed them to her nurse.

From *More Readers Theatre for Beginning Readers* by Suzanne I. Barchers and Charla R. Pfeffinger.
Westport, CT: Libraries Unlimited/Teacher Ideas Press. Copyright © 2006.

Nurse: Now, my dear. Here is what you do. Put on the bearskin. Climb in the cart.

June: Why? Is this a game?

Nurse: You could say that it is a game. You see, I have a magic wand. I am going to show you how to use the wand to stop and start the cart. You can go wherever you want at full speed. Keep the bearskin over you. No one will know who you are.

Narrator One: June took the wand. Soon she was outside in the woods. She flew in the cart for a long time. She felt the sun on her face. She loved the feel of the air on her cheeks.

Narrator Two: June stopped for a rest. She sat under a tree. All of a sudden, she heard some dogs. She put on her bearskin to hide.

Narrator One: The prince from the next kingdom was out hunting. He saw the bear.

Prince: Dogs! Get the bear!

Narrator Two: June saw that the dogs could hurt her. She called out in fear.

June: Call off your dogs! They will kill me!

Narrator One: The prince stopped in shock.

Prince: A bear that talks! What is this?

June: Please don't hurt me. What harm have I done to you?

Prince: Of course, I won't hurt you. Come with me. I will take you to my home.

June: I will come with you. Let me get in my cart.

Narrator Two: The prince watched her get in the cart. She waved the wand. The cart moved down the road.

Narrator One: The prince got on his horse. He rode after her. He did not want to lose sight of her. Soon they were at his castle. The queen met them.

Queen: What have you brought home, son? A bear?

Prince: Yes, Mum.

Queen: What will you do with him?

Prince: This is a most special bear.

Queen: How is that?

Prince: Well, it talks.

Queen: Is that all it can do?

June: That is not all. I will be glad to work for you. I am good at cleaning the house.

Queen: Is that so? Well, let's see.

From *More Readers Theatre for Beginning Readers* by Suzanne I. Barchers and Charla R. Pfeffinger. Westport, CT: Libraries Unlimited/Teacher Ideas Press. Copyright © 2006.

Narrator Two: June was the best helper the queen had ever seen. June worked hard.

Narrator One: One day the prince told the queen about a ball.

Prince: Mum, there is a ball at John's castle. I want to go.

Queen: Of course you may go. Have fun.

June: May I come too? I would like to dance at a ball.

Prince: No! No bear can come to a ball!

Narrator Two: The prince went to the ball. June begged the queen to let her go, too.

June: Please let me go to the ball. I'll hide and just watch. No one will know I am there.

Queen: All right. Just take care that no one sees you.

Narrator One: June ran to the barn. She threw off the bearskin. She touched it with the magic wand. It turned into a silver ball dress. The cart turned into a carriage with two horses. June drove to the ball.

Narrator Two: June went in the castle. She looked so lovely. No one looked as fine as she. The prince saw her and had to dance with her. He could not take his eyes off her.

Narrator One: June drove off at the end of the ball. She wanted to change the dress back to a bearskin right away. The prince rode after her. But he lost sight of her. He went to see the queen.

Prince: Mum, I met a lovely girl. We danced and danced.

Queen: Who is she?

Prince: I don't know her name. We did not talk. She drove off too fast.

Queen: There is a ball in a few nights. You might see her there.

Prince: Yes! If she is there, I will talk with her. I must find out who she is.

Narrator Two: June went to the next ball. She wore a dress of gold. She danced with the prince. But she would not talk with him. When the ball was done, he rode after her. He lost her again.

Narrator One: He told the queen about the dance.

Prince: Mum, I saw her at the ball. We danced and danced.

Queen: Did you find out her name? Did you talk with her?

Prince: No. She would not talk. Mum, I think I am in love with her. What can I do?

Queen: Go to the next ball. She may come to that one.

Narrator Two: June heard the prince and queen talking. She smiled at the prince's words.

From *More Readers Theatre for Beginning Readers* by Suzanne I. Barchers and Charla R. Pfeffinger.
Westport, CT: Libraries Unlimited/Teacher Ideas Press. Copyright © 2006.

Narrator One: June wore a dress of gold and pearls at the third ball. She stunned the prince with her beauty. She would not talk to him. But she let him slip a ring on her finger.

Narrator Two: The prince tried to catch her after the ball. He lost her again. He went to see the queen.

Prince: I think I shall go mad. I am in love with that girl. But I don't know who she is. I danced with her. I gave her a ring. And she ran off. How can I find her?

Queen: Son, calm down. First things first. Tell me all about the ball. Who was there? What did you eat?

Prince: I couldn't eat. All I did was dance.

Queen: Let me get some soup. I'll have the bear bring it to you.

Narrator One: The queen had the cook fix some soup. June put the ring in the bowl. Then she took it to the prince. He ate it slowly. June watched.

Narrator Two: The prince saw the ring. He looked up at the bear.

Prince: The ring! What is going on? Who are you?

Narrator One: June looked at him with kind eyes.

Prince: Take off that bearskin!

Narrator Two: June dropped the bearskin. She wore the dress of gold and pearls.

Prince: It is you! Who are you? Why were you in that bearskin?

June: It is a long story. Let's go see the queen. I would like to tell both of you.

Narrator One: June told them why she had run away. Soon the queen had a plan.

Queen: My son is in love with you. I want you to have time to know him. Maybe you will grow to love him, too. I will send word to your father that you are safe. You can stay here as my guest. How would that work?

Narrator Two: June and the prince agreed to the plan.

Narrator One: And you know how the story ends. June fell in love with the prince. The nurse came to the wedding. And they lived happily ever after.

From *More Readers Theatre for Beginning Readers* by Suzanne I. Barchers and Charla R. Pfeffinger. Westport, CT: Libraries Unlimited/Teacher Ideas Press. Copyright © 2006.

Frank and the Giant

Summary: A poor young shepherd assists a wounded giant who then takes the young man to a party as a reward. There the boy takes a loaf of bread home with him for his next meal. The bread is magical, and each time the boy bites the bread, a gold coin appears in his mouth. Thanks to his good fortune, the shepherd wins the chance of marrying his true love.

Readability: 0.5

Staging: The narrator should stand on the left side of the staging area. The readers should sit on stools in the center of the stage to read their parts.

Props: The giant can be dressed in oversized boots and clothes. The lord and Meg can be dressed richly, with Frank and Mother dressed simply.

Presentation: The giant should have a booming voice. Mother should sound complaining and annoyed with Frank, who should sound confident. Meg should have a pleasant, kind voice.

Characters:

Narrator One

Narrator Two

Frank

Giant

Lord

Mother

Meg

Frank and the Giant

Narrator One: Frank was an orphan. He looked after the sheep of a rich man. This man was a lord. Frank spent day and night in the open fields. One night he heard someone crying. He was shocked to see a giant lying at edge of the woods.

Frank: Who are you?

Giant: I am Borg. I am a giant from far away.

Frank: Are you hurt?

Giant: Yes. I hurt my foot. I fell down while I was trying to pull up an oak tree. Can you bind it for me?

Narrator Two: Frank took off his shirt. He used it to bind up the giant's foot.

Giant: Oh, thank you for helping me. I want to reward you. Follow me.

Frank: Where are we going?

Giant: We are going to a party.

Frank: Is it far away?

Giant: No, but it is deep in the woods.

Frank: I don't think I can go. I need to tend my sheep. I don't want my lord to get mad at me.

Giant: Come on. There's a party going on right now. I promise you will have a lot of fun. Those sheep won't get lost. I promise.

Frank: Well, maybe just for a little while.

Giant: I want you to wear this belt around your waist.

Frank: Why?

Giant: So you'll be invisible. I don't want my brothers to see you. They do not like strangers.

Narrator One: Frank put on the belt. Borg led Frank to a place in the trees where there were hundreds of giants. Frank couldn't believe what he was seeing. There was so much going on. Time passed quickly.

Narrator Two: At midnight one of the giants pulled a large tree out of the ground. All the giants went through a hole to below the ground. Borg looked for Frank before he went down.

Giant: Frank, where are you?

Frank: Here I am, next to you.

Giant: Hold on to me. Then you can come below the ground with us.

From *More Readers Theatre for Beginning Readers* by Suzanne I. Barchers and Charla R. Pfeffinger. Westport, CT: Libraries Unlimited/Teacher Ideas Press. Copyright © 2006.

Narrator One: Frank reached out to the giant. Down they went through the hole in the earth. They entered a big hall. The walls were made of pure gold. The tables were set with more food than Frank had ever seen. Frank ate until he was full. Then he thought about the coming day. He thought about how he would not have any food.

Frank: I will put a loaf of bread under my shirt. No one will miss one loaf of bread.

Narrator Two: He put a full loaf of bread under his shirt.

Giant: Frank, where are you?

Frank: Right here.

Giant: It is time for you to leave. Hold on to me. I'll take you back up to the woods.

Narrator One: Soon Frank was back in the woods. The giant was gone. Frank went back to his sheep. He took off the belt. He hid it carefully in his bag.

Narrator Two: The next morning he was hungry. He tried to cut off a piece of the loaf of bread. The bread wouldn't cut. He tried to bite off a piece of the loaf. To his surprise a piece of gold fell out of his mouth. He bit again. More gold fell out of his mouth. Each time he bit the bread, a piece of gold fell out of his mouth.

Frank: I can't believe how lucky I am. I must hide my loaf of magic bread. I can buy some good things to eat with this gold.

Narrator One: Frank also thought about a young girl named Meg. The lord that Frank worked for was her father. She always smiled at Frank when she saw him. He knew she was only being polite to a poor boy. Still, he had fallen in love with her.

Narrator Two: Frank knew that Meg's birthday was coming soon. For a long time he had wanted to do something special for her. Now he had a plan.

Narrator One: Frank decided he would give her a sack of gold. He wanted it to be a secret gift. If he wore his belt, no one would see him.

Narrator Two: Frank slipped into Meg's room the night before her birthday. He placed the bag of gold on her bed. In the morning, Meg found the bag of gold. She ran to her parents.

Meg: Father! Mother! Look at this bag of gold.

Lord: Where did you get it?

Meg: It was lying on my bed when I woke up this morning.

Mother: Who would leave you a bag of gold?

Meg: Maybe my fairy godmother?

Mother: I don't think so, Meg. I wonder where it came from.

Narrator One: For the next seven nights, Frank put a sack of gold on Meg's bed. Her mother spoke to the lord.

From *More Readers Theatre for Beginning Readers* by Suzanne I. Barchers and Charla R. Pfeffinger.
Westport, CT: Libraries Unlimited/Teacher Ideas Press. Copyright © 2006.

Mother: This is really a strange thing, my dear. You need to find out who is leaving these sacks of gold in Meg's room.

Lord: You are right. How do you think we can do that?

Mother: Tonight you should hide in our daughter's room. Then you can see who is bringing the gold.

Lord: That's a good idea.

Narrator Two: That night a bad storm came up as Frank was leaving. He was going to bring Meg a bag of gold.

Frank: Oh, no! I didn't put on my belt. I'll just take my chances. I think I can slip into Meg's room without being caught. She is always alone. I'm sure I'll be safe.

Narrator One: Meg's father came into the room. He saw Frank with his hand on the bag of gold.

Lord: You stop right there! How dare you try to steal that bag of gold?

Frank: Sir, I, I ….

Lord: I am surprised at you, Frank. I thought you were an honest man. I should send you to prison, but I won't. Pack your things and leave my land now.

Narrator Two: Frank went back to his hut to get his things. He went to the nearest town. He bought himself some fine clothes. He hired a coach with four horses and two servants. He went back to Meg's home.

Frank: Lord, I must speak with you.

Lord: I told you never to come back here again.

Frank: Please, Sir, hear me out. One night I went to the land of giants.

Lord: Frank, I don't want to hear some fairy tale. Just go.

Frank: Please listen to me. When I left the party, I took a loaf of bread. I wanted the loaf to eat the next day. When I tried to cut it, it would not cut. When I tried to bite off a piece, a gold coin would fall out of my mouth.

Lord: Gold coins from bread? I don't believe you!

Frank: It is true. Let me show you.

Narrator One: Frank got out the loaf of bread and bit it. A gold coin fell out of his mouth.

Lord: That is amazing! But why were you in Meg's room?

Frank: I was bringing her a birthday present.

Lord: Why would you do that?

Frank: I have loved her ever since I first saw her. I knew I was not worthy of her when I was poor. Then I had this loaf of magic bread. I knew I could give her something no one else could.

Lord: That is true. Eight sacks of gold are far more than I could give her. So why did you come back?

Frank: I want to ask for her hand in marriage.

Lord: Frank, you are a fine young man. If she wants to marry you, then the answer is yes.

Narrator Two: Frank and Meg—and the loaf of bread—lived happily ever after.

From *More Readers Theatre for Beginning Readers* by Suzanne I. Barchers and Charla R. Pfeffinger.
Westport, CT: Libraries Unlimited/Teacher Ideas Press. Copyright © 2006.

The Fish in the Tree and the Hare in the Stream

Summary: An old man finds a pot of gold. He knows that his wife will tell others about it. He devises a plan. First, he tricks her into thinking fish live in trees and hares live in streams. When she wants to spend their gold, he tries to save the money. She complains to the mayor about him, revealing that she thinks fish live in trees. This leads to her having to obey her husband.

Readability: 0.7

Staging: Place the narrators on one side, the old man and his wife in the middle, and the mayor on the other side.

Props: Have students create an outdoor mural, decorating the stage with plants to portray the woods. The old man and old woman can be dressed in simple clothing. The mayor can be in a suit.

Presentation: The old man should sound patient. The wife should sound quarrelsome. The mayor should sound wise.

Characters:

>Narrator One
>
>Narrator Two
>
>Old Man
>
>Old Woman
>
>Mayor

The Fish in the Tree and the Hare in the Stream

Narrator One: An old man lived with his wife. They could have been happy. But the wife liked to talk a lot. At times, she told tales. She didn't mean to lie. She just liked to talk too much.

Narrator Two: One day the man went to the woods. He stepped into a soft spot. His foot sank.

Old Man: What is this? I think I'll dig a bit.

Narrator One: He dug and dug. He came to a pot.

Old Man: Look at this! It's a pot of gold! Now how can I hide this from my wife? She will want to spend it. She will tell the whole world. Then I will have trouble for sure.

Narrator Two: The old man sat down. He thought and thought.

Old Man: I know what I'll do. First, I'll put the pot of gold back. Then I'll go back to town. I have some shopping to do.

Narrator One: The old man went to town. He bought a big fish and a hare.

Narrator Two: He went back to the woods. He put the fish at the top of a tree.

Narrator One: He tied the hare in a net. He put it by a stream. Then he went home to his wife.

Old Man: Wife! We are in luck!

Old Woman: Why? Tell me about it.

Old Man: No. I can't tell you. You will tell everyone.

Old Woman: No I won't! How can you say that? I won't tell a soul.

Old Man: Well, then. Here is the news. I found a pot of gold in the woods. Now don't tell!

Old Woman: Let me see!

Old Man: I didn't bring it back. I wanted you to be with me.

Old Woman: Let's go get it!

Narrator Two: They went to the woods. On the way, he talked to her.

Old Man: I heard an odd story. I was told that fish now live in trees. And that hares live in streams. Times have changed, my dear.

Old Woman: That is silly. You should not listen to such silly talk.

Old Man: You must be right.

Narrator One: Then the man stopped. He looked up at the tree.

Old Man: Silly talk? Look up in that tree. It looks like a fish is up there!

From *More Readers Theatre for Beginning Readers* by Suzanne I. Barchers and Charla R. Pfeffinger.
Westport, CT: Libraries Unlimited/Teacher Ideas Press. Copyright © 2006.

Old Woman: Oh my! It is a fish! How did a fish get up there?

Old Man: I have no idea. I guess what I heard is true.

Old Woman: Well, don't just stand there! Climb up and get it. We can cook it for dinner.

Narrator Two: The man climbed up the tree. He brought down the fish. They drove on.

Narrator One: Soon they got to the stream. The old man slowed down.

Old Woman: Why are you stopping? Drive on!

Old Man: I see something in a net. It seems to be moving.

Narrator Two: The man ran to the net.

Old Man: Look! It's a hare.

Old Woman: How did a hare get in the net?

Old Man: I have no idea. But there it is.

Old Woman: Well, bring it with us. We can cook it later.

Narrator One: The man took the hare. Then they went to where the pot was buried. They dug it up and went home.

Narrator Two: The man and woman had plenty of money. But the wife was not wise. Each day she asked friends to come and eat with them. She was spending the money on food.

Old Man: Wife, you need to take more care with our gold.

Old Woman: Don't scold me! I want to spend it. You can't stop me.

Old Man: Yes, I can. You can't have another penny.

Old Woman: Is that so? Well, just wait. You won't like what I can do.

Narrator One: The old woman went to the mayor.

Old Woman: Please help me. My husband found some gold.

Mayor: What is wrong with that? That is good news!

Old Woman: He won't share it with me.

Mayor: What does he do with it?

Old Woman: He wants to save it. And he just sits and eats.

Mayor: I will look into it. Let's go see him.

Narrator Two: The mayor went to the old man's house.

Mayor: I hear you have found some gold.

Old Man: Gold? I don't know about gold.

From *More Readers Theatre for Beginning Readers* by Suzanne I. Barchers and Charla R. Pfeffinger.
Westport, CT: Libraries Unlimited/Teacher Ideas Press. Copyright © 2006.

Mayor: Your wife told me. She said you won't share it with her. Now, don't lie to me.

Old Man: She must have dreamed of it. She has such dreams….

Old Woman: What? A dream?

Mayor: Tell us what you saw. That should settle this.

Old Woman: We were in the forest. We saw a fish at the top of a tree.

Mayor: A fish? Is this a joke?

Old Woman: No, no! I'm telling you the truth.

Old Man: See what I mean? A dream.

Old Woman: No! There was a fish! And then we found a hare in the river!

Mayor: Ha! I don't think this was a dream. I think you are daft!

Old Man: Oh no. She just dreams a lot. She talks a lot. She means no harm.

Mayor: Well, I hope not. Can you make sure that she never bothers me again?

Old Man: Of course. She won't bother you again.

Mayor: See that she never does.

Narrator One: The mayor left. The old woman knew that she should not talk so much.

Narrator Two: The old man used the gold to start a shop in the town. The old woman did very well talking and selling their wares. They lived well for the rest of their days.

Narrator One: The old woman learned to talk a bit less. And the old man learned to listen a bit more.

From *More Readers Theatre for Beginning Readers* by Suzanne I. Barchers and Charla R. Pfeffinger.
Westport, CT: Libraries Unlimited/Teacher Ideas Press. Copyright © 2006.

The Little Green Frog

Summary: When the fairies become upset with the kings in a country, they set out to teach them a lesson. One king and one queen will die. Two children are left behind. The fairies raise the daughter, and a grieving father raises his son. When the son is old enough to venture out into the world, the fairies turn the girl into a frog. The frog then tests the young man's ability to follow directions and do as he is told.

Readability: 0.7

Props: Small cup and a mirror

Staging: The narrators should sit on opposite sides of the staging area. Readers should sit on stools or chairs in the middle of the staging area. Those who speak at the beginning of the script should be on the king's left. Prince Leroy should at the king's immediate right with the green frog next to him.

Presentation: The reader for the Green Frog should be able to speak sarcastically when necessary and show her frustration with Leroy's inability to do as she says. Other readers should follow the voice inflection of the characters.

Characters:

Narrator One

Narrator Two

Queen Lily

Wizard

Diana

Rosa

King

Servant

Prince Leroy

Green Frog/Nell

Maiden

The Little Green Frog

Narrator One: Taylor and Troy were both kings. The fairies kept them safe. They were not very nice kings. That's why they needed to be kept safe.

Narrator Two: Taylor was mean to his wife. He was mean to people in the kingdom. He was even mean to his pets. The fairies grew very tired of all this.

Narrator One: Taylor would not change. No one wanted to help when he got sick. He died unhappy and alone. He left behind a baby daughter. She would be the queen when she grew up. Until that day, the fairies took charge of her care. They raised Nell with love.

Narrator Two: Nell's mother became queen. Queen Lily was wise and good. She worked hard to keep the people happy. But she was not happy. She missed Nell.

Queen Lily: Could someone please tell me why the fairies took Nell away from me?

Wizard: My dear, we have gone over this so many times. They feel they have more time to raise Princess Nell. You have so much to do.

Queen Lily: You have said so before. I just don't understand it.

Wizard: Let's look at what you have to do in a day. You have a lot of decisions to make. There is so much fighting going on here. One day a family is fighting. The next day the neighbors are fighting. Then there are the problems with the crops and the—

Queen Lily: Yes, yes, I know. Each day I stop fights and talk to my people. At the end of each day, all my people feel fine again. All but me! I miss Nell.

Wizard: You would have no time to spend with her. It's really better for both of you this way. It won't always be like this.

Narrator One: Many years went by. The fairies still watched over Troy. He loved his wife, Queen Connie. But he often ignored her. Queen Connie caught a chill one cold day. No one could save her. After she died, Troy realized how much he had loved her. He was very sad at losing her.

Narrator Two: Troy had a son, Prince Leroy. By age fifteen, Leroy had learned everything a prince should know. He was charming. He was kind to other people. He was ready for adventure! The fairies had been planning his future.

Diana: Leroy has grown up to be a fine young man. He will be quite a catch.

Rosa: Yes, he would! We must make sure that he and Nell marry. We have planned on that for years.

Diana: But he's a bit too young to marry. We need to make sure he doesn't fall in love with some other girl.

Rosa: Do you have an idea?

Diana: You know that mirror that our aunt left us?

From *More Readers Theatre for Beginning Readers* by Suzanne I. Barchers and Charla R. Pfeffinger.
Westport, CT: Libraries Unlimited/Teacher Ideas Press. Copyright © 2006.

Rosa: You mean the one in the ugly black frame?

Diana: Yes. First, I will cast a spell upon it.

Rosa: What kind of a spell do you want to cast?

Diana: It needs to be a simple one. Let's see. Hmm, I know. We will put the mirror in his room. Each time he looks into it he will see Nell.

Rosa: What a great idea! He will see her face each day. Then he will fall in love with her.

Narrator One: Their plan worked. Each time Leroy looked into the mirror, he saw Nell. He fell madly in love with her. One day he was looking at Nell in the mirror. He could see a young man *and* Nell. Leroy could not believe his eyes! He was sure this young man was with Nell.

Narrator Two: But there was no one with Nell. The fairies wanted to be sure Leroy would not forget Nell.

Narrator One: At last, Leroy turned eighteen years old. His father was very sick. He was near death. The king still missed his wife so much. He told his servants to open the windows and leave. A beautiful bird flew to a window. It sat on the windowsill.

King: Bird, do you sing? Bird, come here.

Narrator Two: The bird flew into the room. Her eyes were fixed on the king's eyes. As he looked at her he started to feel well again. He tried to catch the bird. She flew away. He called in his servants.

King: There was a beautiful bird in my room. I want you to find it. I want it brought back to me.

Servant: What does the bird look like?

Narrator One: He told them all about the bird. Everyone in the palace looked for it. No one could find the bird. The king fell sick again.

Prince Leroy: I can't let my father die. I must find that bird. After all, I am a prince!

Narrator Two: Prince Leroy sent for his friends. They rode north and began to look for the bird. They did not find her.

Prince Leroy: Let us rest for the night. Then we can look south of the palace. I have never been south before. Maybe that is where she lives.

Narrator One: The next day he and his friends rode south. They came to a clearing with bright flowers. There was a bubbling fountain with clear water. Leroy was quite thirsty. He stopped to get a drink.

Narrator Two: Leroy always had a cup with him. He took it from his pocket. He started to dip it in the water. A little green frog jumped onto the rim of the cup.

Narrator One: Leroy tried to shake it off his cup. It did no good. As soon as he shook the frog off the cup, it jumped back. He looked into the frog's eyes. He knew he had seen them before. He just couldn't remember where. Can you guess whose eye's they were? [*pause*] Of course, they were Nell's eyes.

Green Frog: Please, drink the water. Then I will tell you how to find the bird you are looking for.

Prince Leroy: All right. Where can I find this bird?

Green Frog: You must listen and do just what I say. You are to go down that road alone.

Prince Leroy: Which road?

Green Frog: The road where the large trees stand. Walk all day long. Then you will come to a castle.

Prince Leroy: Who lives there?

Green Frog: You do not need to know. It does not matter.

Prince Leroy: Then why am I going there?

Green Frog: If you will just listen, you will find out! Take this tiny grain of sand. Put it into the ground when you get to the gate of the castle. It will open the gate. Everyone inside will fall asleep. Go at once to the stable. Choose the most handsome horse. Jump on its back. Come back to me as fast as you can. Good-bye, prince. I wish you good luck.

Prince Leroy: Wait! Don't go back into the water! That's it? Just get a horse? [*pause*] Well, I guess it would be a good idea to get a fresh horse. Mine is quite tired, after all.

Narrator Two: The prince did just as he had been told. Well, almost. Leroy had his hand on the finest horse in the stable. He saw a splendid harness on the wall. He thought it belonged to the horse. Without thinking, he put it on the horse's back. Suddenly, everyone woke up. The stable hands saw the prince. They grabbed him. They took him to their ruler.

Ruler: What were you doing in my stable?

Prince Leroy: I was taking a horse.

Ruler: You were stealing one of my horses? You admit this?

Prince Leroy: Yes. I have a very good reason.

Ruler: I would really like to hear it.

Narrator One: Leroy told him all about his father, the bird, and the frog.

Ruler: That is a pretty poor excuse, young man. So poor, it must be true.

Prince Leroy: Yes it is, sir. It would be hard to make that up.

Ruler: I believe you. Take the horse and go on your way.

From *More Readers Theatre for Beginning Readers* by Suzanne I. Barchers and Charla R. Pfeffinger.
Westport, CT: Libraries Unlimited/Teacher Ideas Press. Copyright © 2006.

Narrator Two: Leroy went back to the fountain. He wanted to talk to the frog.

Green Frog: Well, I see you came back. But you didn't listen to what I told you to do. I am not happy with you.

Prince Leroy: I am so sorry. I just thought that the harness belonged on the horse and—

Green Frog: Okay, okay. I know what you thought. Let's try another plan to get the bird. Here is a nugget of gold. Do just as you did before. But don't go into the stable. Go into the castle. Go down the hall to a room filled with perfume. There you will find a beautiful maiden asleep on a bed. Wake her. Bring her here. Do not stop for anything.

Narrator One: Prince Leroy did as the frog told him. He found the maiden and woke her up.

Prince Leroy: Come with me. Quickly!

Maiden: I am not sure I should.

Prince Leroy: Please. It is very important. We must leave the castle now.

Maiden: May I put on my slippers first?

Prince Leroy: Well, I guess so. We need to go quickly.

Narrator Two: Once again, he had not done as he was told. He was captured. The ruler wouldn't even listen to him. Leroy was tied up and on his way to prison. The fairies had to free him. He went back to the fountain and faced the frog. He knew he had failed again.

Green Frog: I bet you have never done as you were told. You have been spoiled all of your life.

Prince Leroy: You are right. Won't you please give me another chance?

Green Frog: Okay, go back to the castle. Bury this small diamond close to the gate. Don't go near the stable or into the palace. Walk straight to the garden. Go through the gate. Follow the path to a small forest.
   There you will find a tree with a trunk of gold and leaves of emeralds. You will see the beautiful bird sitting on a branch. Cut off that branch. Bring the bird and the branch back to me quickly. But I warn you! Do as I tell you. I will not help you again.

Narrator One: It was hard but this time he did as he was told. He even ignored the truly splendid golden birdcage. He returned to the fountain. It was gone! Instead there was a palace. Nell stood in the doorway. Leroy was quite confused.

Prince Leroy: Where did you come from?

Nell: I have been here all along.

Prince Leroy: How can that be? The only thing I have seen here is a frog.

Nell: That's true.

From *More Readers Theatre for Beginning Readers* by Suzanne I. Barchers and Charla R. Pfeffinger. Westport, CT: Libraries Unlimited/Teacher Ideas Press. Copyright © 2006.

Prince Leroy: So where were you? And who are you?

Nell: I'll tell you all that I know. It won't take long. I do not know anything about my country or my parents. The only thing I know for sure is my name. I am called Nell.

Prince Leroy: That's very strange. Someone should know who you are.

Nell: No. I have always lived in alone. The fairies have taken care of me. They insist on being obeyed. That is why they changed the little house into the fountain and changed me into a frog.

Prince Leroy: Why did they think you needed to be a frog?

Nell: Would you have listened to me if I had not been a frog?

Prince Leroy: I guess not.

Nell: I wanted you to find the bird. Not just for yourself, but also for me.

Prince Leroy: Why is that?

Nell: I had to stay a frog until you found that bird. Why do you want that bird?

Prince Leroy: My father is very ill. He's been sick ever since my mother's died. One day this bird came into his room. It made him feel better. When it flew away, he fell ill again.

Nell: Oh, how sad. You're a king's son?

Prince Leroy: Yes, King Troy is my father.

Nell: That's too bad.

Prince Leroy: Why do you say that?

Nell: I like you a lot, but we are not equals.

Prince Leroy: I like you too, Nell. I am sure we are meant to be good friends. Maybe even husband and wife.

Nell: That could never happen.

Prince Leroy: Yes it could!

Nell: How can you say that?

Prince Leroy: Do you believe in fate?

Nell: I guess so.

Prince Leroy: One day a mirror appeared in my room. When I looked into it, I saw you. For years I have watched you in that mirror.

Nell: That sounds like something the fairies would do. I don't think this is fate.

Prince Leroy: You may be right.

Nell: Maybe I should go ask the fairies what they have been up to.

Narrator Two: Just then a coach pulled up beside them. Inside were Diana, Rosa, and a beautiful woman. The bird flew onto Leroy's shoulder.

Nell: Fairies, I believe I have done all that you have asked me to do.

Diana: Yes, you have, dear. We are quite proud of you.

Nell: I would like you to tell me what is going on. And I want to know who my parents are.

Rosa: And why do you need to know this?

Nell: Because I have fallen in love with Prince Leroy. If we are not equals, I cannot see him any more.

Diana: Then I guess it is time to tell you the truth. Your father was a king. He died long ago. Queen Lily is your mother, Nell.

Prince Leroy: Then we are equals. We can get married, Nell!

Nell: If we truly fall in love.

Rosa: And if your parents approve.

Queen Lily: I am sure that won't be a problem.

Diana: We must go to your father, Prince Leroy. Get into the coach. I will send word to your father that the bird has been found.

Narrator One: Soon the coach was at the palace. The king was still quite sick. He was lying outside so he could feel the sun on his face. Everyone was sure he would die at any time.

Narrator Two: The bird flew from the coach. She went right to the king. Once she was near him, the king felt better. Then, the bird changed back into her true form. Can you guess who she was? [*pause*] The bird was his wife, Queen Connie.

Narrator One: Prince Leroy had learned an important lesson. He knew he needed to treat Nell with love and respect. And when they were truly in love, Prince Leroy asked for her hand in marriage. And she said,

Nell: Of course I'll marry you.

Bobino

Summary: Bobino's father sends him away to be tutored. Bobino returns, knowing only how to understand the language of the animals. His disappointed father intends to have him killed. A sympathetic servant alerts him to the truth, and Bobino runs away. While traveling, he helps out others and eventually is made king of a foreign land.

Readability: 0.8

Staging: The narrators can stand to one side. Have the merchant stand next to the narrator, with Bobino next to him. The Merchant can leave the stage after his part. Have the other characters on the other side of Bobino.

Props: The stage can look like a road.

Presentation: Consider having Bobino move across the stage as he speaks to the different characters.

Characters:

Narrator One

Narrator Two

Bobino

Merchant

Man One

Man Two

Herdsman

Peasant

Man Three

Man Four

Bobino

Narrator One: A merchant had a son name Bobino. The son was smart. He loved to learn new things.

Narrator Two: The merchant sent him to a teacher. He thought Bobino would learn a lot. Years passed. Bobino came home at last.

Bobino: I'm home!

Merchant: Tell me, son. What was it like for you? Did you do well with your studies?

Bobino: Yes, I did.

Merchant: Well, it is good to have you home.

Narrator One: One day they were out for a walk. The birds chirped in the trees. Bobino and the merchant could hardly hear each other speak.

Merchant: Those birds are so loud! I hate the noise they make.

Bobino: I like them.

Merchant: Well, I don't. I wish they would stop.

Bobino: Do you want to know what they are saying?

Merchant: What can you mean? How can you tell that?

Bobino: I learned how they talk.

Merchant: Is that what I paid for? To have you learn how to hear what the animals say? I thought you would learn about things like how to speak French.

Bobino: This is where my teacher thought I should start. I can learn more next year.

Narrator Two: The two of them went home. The dog met them. He was barking loudly.

Bobino: Do you want to know what he is saying?

Merchant: Let me be. Don't bother me. I have wasted my money.

Narrator One: Later, they sat down to dinner. The frogs in the pond began to croak. They were very loud.

Merchant: These frogs must stop!

Bobino: Do you want to know what they are saying?

Merchant: No! Be off with you. Go to bed. I don't want to see you again!

Narrator Two: Bobino went to bed. His father was so mad. He sent for two men. He told them what to do. One of the men woke him up the next day. The man was very sad.

Bobino: Why are you here? And why do you look so sad?

Man One: Your father is mad at you. He wants you dead. I am taking you to be killed.

Bobino: Why does he want me dead? What have I done to him?

Man Two: You have done no wrong. He is mad because you learned how the animals talk. He thought you would learn much more.

Bobino: Then kill me now. Why wait?

Man One: I don't want to see you dead. I would rather risk having your father be mad at me.

Man Two: I know what to do. A deer was killed last night. Let's take its heart back to your father. He will think it is yours. You can get away.

Bobino: Thank you. You are both so kind to me.

Narrator One: Bobino walked out to the woods. He walked all day. Soon he came to a house. He asked for a place to sleep. The man of the house asked him in.

Herdsman: Come in. You may stay here with us. Share some food with us.

Narrator Two: The dog began to bark. Bobino listened for a bit.

Bobino: Send your wife and daughters to bed. Then get ready. A band of robbers is on the way.

Herdsman: How do you know this? Who told you this?

Bobino: The dog told me. I know what he is saying. Listen to me. You will be glad you did.

Herdsman: I trust you.

Narrator One: After some time, the clock struck twelve. The herdsman and Bobino heard footsteps. They were ready. They sprang on the robbers. They hit them with clubs. The robbers ran away.

Herdsman: Thank you! I owe you a lot. Will you stay with me?

Bobino: No. I need to keep going. I will leave when it is light out.

Narrator Two: Bobino walked away the next morning. He walked all day. That night he came to a man's house. He started to knock on the door.

Narrator One: Then he saw something odd. Four frogs were throwing a small bottle back and forth. They croaked as they threw it. Bobino listened to them. Then he knocked at the door.

Peasant: Who are you? What do you want?

Bobino: I have been walking all day. I need a place to stay for the night.

Peasant: Come in. Come in. Join us for supper.

Narrator Two: During supper, Bobino learned that the man's daughter was sick.

From *More Readers Theatre for Beginning Readers* by Suzanne I. Barchers and Charla R. Pfeffinger. Westport, CT: Libraries Unlimited/Teacher Ideas Press. Copyright © 2006.

Peasant: I fear my daughter will never get well again. A doctor sent some medicine. But his servant lost it.

Bobino: I think I can help you.

Peasant: How can you help?

Bobino: I know what the animals are saying. Some frogs were tossing a bottle back and forth. I think it may be what you need.

Peasant: That could be! Let's try to find it.

Narrator One: They found the bottle in the ditch. The next day the girl was much better.

Peasant: What can I do to thank you?

Bobino: Nothing. I will be on my way.

Peasant: Please. Stay. I owe you so much.

Narrator Two: Bobino went on his way. One day he stopped to rest. He was near two men. He could hear them talking.

Bobino: Where are you going?

Man Three: We are on our way to town.

Man Four: A new king is to be chosen.

Narrator One: Some birds in the tree began to talk.

Bobino: Can you hear the birds?

Man Three: Yes. So?

Bobino: They say one of us will be the new king.

Man Four: You are a fool. Go on …

Narrator Two: Bobino went on his way. Soon he came to the town. A great crowd was there.

Narrator One: The new king would be chosen by an eagle. It was to be let loose from a cage. It would be watched until it landed. Wherever it landed—that would be the new king.

Narrator Two: The eagle was let go. It flew right to Bobino. All the people shouted. Bobino was to be the new ruler.

Narrator One: Bobino was happy with his new role. He was a wise ruler for the rest of his life.

From *More Readers Theatre for Beginning Readers* by Suzanne I. Barchers and Charla R. Pfeffinger. Westport, CT: Libraries Unlimited/Teacher Ideas Press. Copyright © 2006.

Cat and Mouse, Friends Forever

Summary: A sly cat decides to make friends with a mouse. Although her motives seem honorable, in the end the true nature of the selfish cat comes through.

Readability: 0.8

Staging: The narrators should stand on the either side of the staging area. Have the cat sit on a high stool near Narrator One, who will be indicating sound effects. Have the mouse sit on a lower stool by Narrator Two.

Props: The stage can be set up to look like a house, with a pot in a corner.

Presentation: Have students practice the meows and squeaks. If preferred, divide these parts among the audience members.

Characters:

Narrator One

Narrator Two

Audience

Cat

Mouse

Cat and Mouse, Friends Forever

Narrator One: Once upon a time there were a cat and a mouse. They became great friends.

Narrator Two: Now we all know that cats and mice are not great friends. So why do you think this cat wanted the mouse for a friend?

Narrator One: Let's find out. But first, everyone has to help with this story. So when I raise my hand, everyone should say *meow, meow, meow*. Ready?

Audience *(Narrator One raises hand):* Meow, meow, meow.

Narrator Two: When I raise my hand, everyone should say *squeak, squeak, squeak*. Let's try it.

Audience *(Narrator Two raises hand):* Squeak, squeak, squeak.

Narrator One: And now, to our story.

Cat: Why don't you come and live with me in my house, Mouse?

Audience *(Narrator One raises hand):* Meow, meow, meow.

Mouse: Do you really think that is such a good idea, Cat?

Audience *(Narrator Two raises hand):* Squeak, squeak, squeak.

Cat: Of course. We are such good friends. I know we will get along just fine.

Mouse: Maybe you are right. But I think we need some rules.

Cat: Rules? What for?

Mouse: So we both know what each of us is to do. Like who cleans up. Things like that.

Cat: Okay. Why don't we split up the work? We can each have our own chores.

Mouse: That is fine with me. What else do we need to plan for?

Cat: We must store food for the winter. Food can be hard to find then.

Mouse: That's true. I have an idea. You are good at hunting. You can look for food. I'll do the cleaning.

Cat: That's wise, little mouse. You could run into a trap. Then it would be all over for you. I will take care of getting the food.

Audience *(Narrator One raises hand):* Meow, meow, meow.

Audience *(Narrator Two raises hand):* Squeak, squeak, squeak.

Narrator Two: Soon it was fall. The cat and mouse decided they should buy a little pot of fat. They would save it for the winter.

Mouse: Where do you think we should keep our pot of fat?

From *More Readers Theatre for Beginning Readers* by Suzanne I. Barchers and Charla R. Pfeffinger. Westport, CT: Libraries Unlimited/Teacher Ideas Press. Copyright © 2006.

Cat: I think we should put it in the church. No one would steal it from there.

Mouse: Where will you hide it?

Cat: I'll hide it in a corner. But we need to save it for winter when we are hungry.

Narrator One: So the cat hid the little pot of fat in the church. Before long, he wanted a taste of the fat. He made up an excuse to go out.

Cat: My cousin has a new little son, white with brown spots. She wants me to be its godmother. I am going to go out today to see it. Can you take care of the housework alone today?

Mouse: Yes. Maybe they will have some food. Bring me a few crumbs of food if you can.

Narrator Two: The cat went straight to the church. She found the little pot of fat. She began to lick it. She licked off the top of the fat in the pot.

Audience *(Narrator One raises hand):* Meow, meow, meow.

Cat: I feel so fat! I think I will take a walk along the roofs of the town.

Audience *(Narrator One raises hand):* Meow, meow, meow.

Narrator One: After a walk, the cat stretched herself out in the sun. She took a long nap. It was dark by the time she got home.

Mouse: Ah, here you are! You must certainly have had a good day.

Cat: It was fine. I am sorry I couldn't bring you any crumbs.

Mouse: Oh that's all right. What is the kitty's name?

Cat: Ahhh. Top Off.

Mouse: Top Off! That is an odd name. Is it a family name?

Cat: No. What is odd about the name? It is no worse than Breadthief, as your godchild is called.

Mouse: I guess you're right. Well, it's time to sleep. Good night, dear Cat.

Audience *(Narrator Two raises hand):* Squeak, squeak, squeak.

Cat: Good night.

Audience *(Narrator One raises hand):* Meow, meow, meow.

Narrator Two: A few days passed. The cat wanted some more of the fat from the pot.

Cat: Can you take care of the house today? There is another new kitten. They want me to be godmother.

Mouse: Of course you must go. Have a good time.

Narrator One: The cat sneaked to the church. Then she ate up half of the pot of fat.

From *More Readers Theatre for Beginning Readers* by Suzanne I. Barchers and Charla R. Pfeffinger. Westport, CT: Libraries Unlimited/Teacher Ideas Press. Copyright © 2006.

Cat: It is fine to eat alone. This is the best fat!

Audience *(Narrator One raises hand):* Meow, meow, meow.

Narrator Two: The cat felt good. She took a long nap like before. It was dark when she went home.

Mouse: Welcome home, Cat. Tell me, what is the name of the new kitten?

Cat: Half Gone.

Mouse: Half Gone! What an odd name!

Cat: My cousins like it. That's what counts.

Mouse: Top Off! Half Gone! They make me wonder.

Cat: Wonder? About what?

Mouse: Oh, nothing really. Nothing …

Cat: Mouse, you sit at home all day and think too much.

Mouse: You know I can't get out much. Well, it's time to sleep. Good night, dear cat.

Audience *(Narrator Two raises hand):* Squeak, squeak, squeak.

Cat: Good night.

Audience *(Narrator One raises hand):* Meow, meow, meow.

Narrator Two: A few days passed. The cat wanted some of the last of the fat from the pot.

Cat: Mouse, all good things come in threes. I have been asked to be a godmother for another kitten. The kitten is quite black. It has very white paws.

Mouse: I wonder what they will name this kitten.

Cat: I don't know.

Narrator One: The mouse stayed home and cleaned.

Narrator Two: The cat ate the last of the pot of fat.

Cat: Such a pity the pot was so small. Now the fat is all gone.

Narrator One: This time the cat stayed out very late. When she came home the mouse was up waiting for her.

Mouse: How nice of you to come home. By the way, what is the name of your third godchild?

Cat: Ah. He is called Clean Gone.

Mouse: Clean Gone! I do not believe you. That isn't a real name. Clean Gone, my foot!

Cat: Mouse, it sounds like you don't trust me.

Mouse: Well, you must admit those are odd names. I can't help but wonder what they really mean.

Narrator Two: The cat shook her head. She curled up and went to sleep. The pot of fat was empty. So there was no reason for the cat to go out.

Narrator One: Soon it was the middle of winter. There was no food to be found. The mouse thought about their pot of fat.

Mouse: Cat, I am so hungry. We must go get our pot of fat that you hid in the church. It will really taste very good right now.

Cat: Yes, it would taste good.

Narrator Two: They went right to the church.

Mouse: Where is the pot of fat, Cat?

Cat: In that corner, over there.

Mouse: There is a pot. But it is empty, Cat.

Cat: But how can that be? I was sure this would be a safe place to hide it.

Mouse: Safe! It would have been safe from others. But it wasn't safe from you.

Cat: What do you mean?

Mouse: No one else knew where the pot of fat was but you. Now the fat is gone.

Cat: Someone else may have found it.

Mouse: I don't think so. And you say you are a true friend to me! But you are not. You are selfish. And you are a liar.

Cat: How can you say such mean things to me?

Mouse: Because I am not stupid. You ate the fat when you said you were going to be a godmother. The first godchild was really the top off of the pot. The second godchild wasn't real. You meant you had eaten the pot half gone. Then you came back for the third time. That's when you ate the pot—

Cat: Will you be quiet! If you say another word I will eat you as well.

Narrator One: The poor mouse couldn't stop himself. The words *clean gone* were already on the tip of his tongue.

Mouse: Clean Gone!

Audience *(Narrator Two raises hand):* Squeak, squeak, squeak.

Cat: I warned you.

From *More Readers Theatre for Beginning Readers* by Suzanne I. Barchers and Charla R. Pfeffinger. Westport, CT: Libraries Unlimited/Teacher Ideas Press. Copyright © 2006.

Narrator Two: The cat grabbed the mouse in one paw. She swallowed him whole.

Narrator One: We all knew cats and mice couldn't really be friends. Didn't we?

Audience *(Narrator One raises hand):* Meow, meow, meow.

From *More Readers Theatre for Beginning Readers* by Suzanne I. Barchers and Charla R. Pfeffinger.
Westport, CT: Libraries Unlimited/Teacher Ideas Press. Copyright © 2006.

Part 2

First-Grade Scripts

The Flower Queen's Daughter

Summary: In this adaptation of an Austrian tale, a prince saves an old woman who has fallen into a ditch. She rewards him with a magical bell that calls forth helpers. If he can succeed, he can marry the Flower Queen's daughter. Use this script to discuss why perennial flowers die back during the winter.

Readability: 1.2

Staging: Narrators should stand on one side of the staging area. Other readers should sit in the back of the staging area and move forward to the center to speak during narration. The prince should remain in the center at all times.

Props: Have a student offstage ring a bell at the appropriate times.

Presentation: Readers should use voices appropriate to the parts.

Characters:

Narrator One

Narrator Two

Old Woman

Prince Kyle

Old Man

Adam

Sam

Dragon Mother

Princess

Flower Queen

The Flower Queen's Daughter

Narrator One: Prince Kyle was riding his horse through a meadow. He came to a deep open ditch. He heard crying sounds from the ditch. He got down from his horse. He found an old woman in the ditch.

Old Woman: Please, help me out of here.

Narrator Two: Kyle bent down and lifted her out.

Prince Kyle: How did you end up in this ditch?

Old Woman: I went to the market to sell my eggs. I lost my way when it got dark. I fell into this ditch. I am so glad you found me.

Prince Kyle: You cannot walk much. Let me put you on my horse. I'll take you home. Where do you live?

Old Woman: I live in a little hut. It is near the woods.

Narrator One: Soon they came to the hut.

Old Woman: You have a kind heart. Let me give you a gift. There is someone you should meet. She's a lovely young woman.

Prince Kyle: Who is she?

Old Woman: She is the daughter of the Queen of the Flowers. A dragon keeps her in his care. You must set her free. I can help you do that. Just wait a moment. [*pause*] Here is a little bell to help you.

Prince Kyle: How will this bell help me?

Old Woman: Listen. Ring it once. The King of the Eagles will come to help you. Ring it twice. The King of the Foxes will come to help you. Ring it three times. The King of the Fishes will come to help you.

Narrator Two: The old woman gave him the bell. Then she and her hut vanished.

Prince Kyle: She must have been a good fairy.

Narrator One: He put the bell in his coat. Then he rode home. The next day he began to look for the princess. He looked for a year. One day he met an old man.

Prince Kyle: I am looking for the daughter of the Flower Queen. She is with the dragon. Do you know where he lives?

Old Man: No, I don't. Check with my father. His name is Adam. He lives down the road. He is a long way away. But he may be able to help you.

Prince Kyle: How far away does he live?

Old Man: It will take a full year to get to his hut.

Prince Kyle: I have looked for a year. I guess I can keep looking. Thank you for your help.

From *More Readers Theatre for Beginning Readers* by Suzanne I. Barchers and Charla R. Pfeffinger.
Westport, CT: Libraries Unlimited/Teacher Ideas Press. Copyright © 2006.

Narrator One: Kyle walked down the road for a year. Then he found Adam.

Prince Kyle: You are Adam, right?

Adam: Yes, I am. Who sent you?

Prince Kyle: Your son.

Adam: Then I will help you. What do you want?

Prince Kyle: I am looking for the daughter of the Flower Queen. The dragon is keeping her. Do you know where he lives?

Adam: No. But go down this road for a year. You will find my father, Sam. I know he can help you.

Narrator Two: Prince Kyle went down the road for a third year. At last he reached a hut. He met an old man.

Prince Kyle: Are you Sam?

Sam: Yes, I am. What do you want?

Prince Kyle: Your son said you could tell me where the dragon lives.

Sam: He lives on the top of that hill. You are in luck.

Prince Kyle: Why is that?

Sam: He has just begun his year of sleep.

Prince Kyle: His year of sleep?

Sam: Yes. For one whole year he stays awake. The next year he sleeps. Go to the top of the second hill. The dragon's mother is up there. She has a dance each night. The princess will be there. Good luck to you.

Narrator One: Prince Kyle went up to the top of the second hill. There was a castle. It was made of gold. It had windows with lots of jewels. He opened the gate. Seven dragons rushed at him. They asked him what he wanted.

Prince Kyle: I have heard that the dragon's mother is kind. I would like to work for her.

Narrator Two: This pleased them. The oldest took him to meet the mother. She was seated on the throne. She was the ugliest woman he had seen. On top of that, she had three heads! Her voice sounded like a croaking raven.

Dragon Mother: Why are you here?

Prince Kyle: I would like to work for you.

Dragon Mother: Very well. I have a job for you. First, lead my horse out to the field. Look after her. Bring her home at night. If she is not safe, you will pay with your life.

Prince Kyle: I can do that.

Narrator Two: As soon as Prince Kyle led the horse into the field, she vanished. Prince Kyle looked and looked for her. He couldn't find her. He sat down on a big stone. Then he saw an eagle flying over his head. He took out the bell. He rang it once. In a moment the King of the Eagles landed at his feet.

King of the Eagles: I know you are looking for Dragon Mother's horse. She is running in the clouds. I will call all the eagles of the air. They will catch her and bring her to you.

Narrator One: The King of the Eagles flew away. That night Prince Kyle looked up in the sky. He saw thousands of eagles driving the horse toward him. They landed at his feet and gave him the horse. Prince Kyle took her home. Dragon Mother was surprised to see them.

Dragon Mother: You did well. You shall come to my dance. You must wear this coat. It is made of copper.

Narrator Two: Prince Kyle went into a big room. Some dragons were dancing. Soon he saw the princes.

Prince Kyle: Will you dance with me?

Princess: Yes, I will.

Prince Kyle: [*whisper*] I have come to free you!

Princess: That will not be easy. I know you passed the first day of Dragon Mother's test. Bring her horse back two more times. Then ask her to give you a foal.

Narrator One: The next morning, Prince Kyle led the horse out into the field. She disappeared in front of him. He took out his bell and rang it twice. The King of the Foxes stood in front of him.

King of Foxes: I know what you want. I will call all the foxes of the world. They will find the horse. She is hiding on a hill.

Narrator Two: The king of the foxes disappeared. The next night, the foxes brought the horse to the prince. He rode her home to Dragon Mother.

Dragon Mother: You did well. It is almost time for the dance. Wear this coat made of silver. Shall we go?

Narrator One: She led him to the dance. The princess was happy to see him.

Prince Kyle: Will you dance with me?

Princess: Oh, yes. I am so glad you are safe. I hope you do well again. Be sure to ask for her horse's foal.

Prince Kyle: Why do I want the foal?

Princess: Once you have the foal, we can escape. Take it to the field after the dance. Wait for me there. We can ride away on her.

From *More Readers Theatre for Beginning Readers* by Suzanne I. Barchers and Charla R. Pfeffinger.
Westport, CT: Libraries Unlimited/Teacher Ideas Press. Copyright © 2006.

Narrator Two: On the third day Prince Kyle led the horse to the field. Once more she vanished. Prince Kyle took out his bell. He rang it three times. The King of the Fishes appeared.

King of the Fishes: I know what you want me to do. The horse is hiding in a river. I will ask all the fishes of the sea to bring it back.

Narrator One: That night, the horse was back. He led her home.

Dragon Mother: You did well, Prince. What shall I give you as a reward?

Prince Kyle: Could I have a foal from your horse?

Dragon Mother: All right. And here is a coat of gold to wear to the dance.

Narrator Two: That evening he came to the dance in his golden coat. After a while, Kyle slipped away. He went to the stables. There he mounted his foal. He rode out into the field to wait for the princess. Soon she came to the meadow. He put her on his horse. They flew like the wind. Soon they reached the Flower Queen's dwelling. On the way, they fell in love.

Flower Queen: Thank you for returning my daughter, Prince Kyle. Is there anything I can give you as a reward?

Prince Kyle: I wish to marry your daughter.

Flower Queen: And do you want to marry him, my dear?

Princess: Yes, I do.

Flower Queen: I will let you marry. But she can stay with you only in the summer. In winter she must live with me in my palace under the ground.

Prince Kyle: Then that is what we will do.

Narrator Two: Prince Kyle took her to his home. There they were married. They lived happily until winter came. Then the princess left to join her mother under the ground.

Narrator One: In the summer she lived with her husband.

Narrator Two: Why do you think the she has to go under the ground in the winter?

Narrator One *(pause for audience to respond):* And this was how it went all of their lives.

The Proud Apple Branch

Summary: In 1872, Hans Christian Andersen wrote a fairy tale about a conceited apple branch. The branch sees itself as one of the beautiful plants. But after a conversation with a sunbeam about the dandelion the branch has always considered ugly, the branch realizes everyone sees beauty differently.

Readability: 1.3

Staging: Narrators should be on one side of the stage. The other readers should sit on chairs in the back of the stage. They should move forward when they read.

Props: None

Presentation: Voice inflection should reflect the script.

Characters:

Narrator One

Spring

Narrator Two

Ana

Jack

Apple Branch

Sunbeam

The Proud Apple Branch

Narrator One: It was May. The wind still blew cold. The trees, fields, and flowers knew spring had come. She seemed quite busy. Buds were popping out. Grass was growing. Even the weeds were showing off their flowers.

Spring: This apple tree has so many pink blossoms. It is so pretty. Oh, look. There is a coach. I wonder why it is stopping here.

Narrator Two: A young woman was in the coach. She and her friends were coming home from town.

Ana: That tree is so pretty. I think I'll take a branch home.

Jack: Let me cut one off for you. What are you going to do with it?

Ana: I will put it in the vase in the living room.

Narrator One: Ana took the branch home. She put it in a clear vase. She added some fresh twigs from a beech tree. It was so pretty. Everyone who came into the room looked at it. Some people talked a lot about it. Others said very little. The apple branch was rather vain. It thought everyone should talk about how pretty it was.

Apple Branch: Some of these humans are such bores!

Sunbeam: Are you talking to me?

Apple Branch: No. I was just talking.

Sunbeam: Why do you think these humans are bores?

Apple Branch: Listen to them talk. They are just like some of the plants in the garden.

Sunbeam: What do you mean?

Apple Branch: Some flowers and plants have beautiful colors. They are just like me. Others are so dull, just like the bores in this room. I am so glad I am one of the beautiful ones.

Narrator Two: The apple branch looked outside. It took great pity on the dandelions.

Apple Branch: Look at those poor dandelions. It is not their fault that they are so ugly. They have such a boring name, too. I guess humans are just like us. We all have to be different.

Sunbeam: Plants may look different. But each of them is beautiful in its own way.

Apple Branch: How can you say all plants are beautiful? Some of them are just ugly! Look at that dandelion.

Sunbeam: You are looking at the outside of things. You have to look on the inside. That is where you will find the good.

Apple Branch: I am sure there isn't much good on the inside of the dandelion.

Sunbeam: Why do you pick on it?

From *More Readers Theatre for Beginning Readers* by Suzanne I. Barchers and Charla R. Pfeffinger. Westport, CT: Libraries Unlimited/Teacher Ideas Press. Copyright © 2006.

Apple Branch: No one ever puts a dandelion in a vase. It is often stepped on. It has flowers like wool.

Sunbeam: Those are its seeds.

Apple Branch: Seeds? It doesn't matter what you want to call them. They blow away in little pieces all over the place. They are just weeds.

Sunbeam: There is nothing wrong with weeds.

Apple Branch: I am just glad that I am not one of them.

Narrator One: Just then the apple branch saw a group of children outside. They sat among the yellow dandelions in the garden. One child kicked his legs as he rolled in the dandelions. He laughed aloud with joy.

Sunbeam: Did you see that? He does not care that it is a weed.

Apple Branch: He is just a child.

Narrator Two: One of the girls broke off some of the flowers. She left long stems on them. She bent the stems so they formed links. She made a chain for her neck. One of the boys made a wreath to wear around his head. They were having a lot of fun.

Sunbeam: Look at what those children are doing. I think they are very clever. They look so cute wearing those flowers. You can't do that with just any flower.

Apple Branch: Why not?

Sunbeam: Adults don't mind if children play with them. But they get very upset if the children pick the garden flowers. Look at what that girl is picking.

Narrator One: All the blossoms had turned to seeds. She held them gently in a white bouquet. They looked like fine snowy feathers.

Narrator Two: She gave each child a stem. The children held them up to their mouths. With one puff of breath they tried to blow away the seeds.

Sunbeam: Now do you see the beauty of dandelions? They give so much pleasure.

Apple Branch: Yes, to children. But children enjoy simple things. They don't always care about real beauty.

Narrator One: Soon an old woman came into the garden. She began to dig in the ground.

Sunbeam: Do you see that woman out there? She is digging up the dandelion plants.

Apple Branch: Yes. Good for her! Someone needs to get rid of those weeds.

Sunbeam: You have a lot to learn, don't you? She is not trying to get rid of them. She is going to use those roots.

Apple Branch: Use them? How silly!

From *More Readers Theatre for Beginning Readers* by Suzanne I. Barchers and Charla R. Pfeffinger. Westport, CT: Libraries Unlimited/Teacher Ideas Press. Copyright © 2006.

Sunbeam: It's not silly at all. She will boil some for tea. The rest she will sell. Then she will have money to buy other things. There is more to the dandelion than just what you see.

Apple Branch: I guess so. But beauty is still better.

Sunbeam: You have a right to think that.

Narrator Two: Just then Ana and her friends came into the room. She had two large leaves in her hand. She carefully took away the leaves. There was a seed crown from a dandelion plant.

Ana: See this pretty flower? I'll put it in here with the apple branch.

Apple Branch: I can't believe it! I am going to be stuck in this vase next to a dandelion. How dare she put that thing next to me?

Sunbeam: It's not just a dandelion to Ana.

Apple Branch: Why would she do this?

Sunbeam: Shhh, listen to her talking to her friends. Maybe you will learn something.

Ana: I am going to paint a picture of the three of them together. Everyone sees the beauty in an apple branch. There is a different kind of beauty in this flower. They will make a wonderful painting.

Narrator One: The sunbeam kissed the lowly weed. Then she kissed the apple blossom branch.

Sunbeam: Now do you understand?

Apple Branch: I guess so. But the dandelion? It's so common.

Sunbeam: Yes, it is. It doesn't try to be something it isn't. That's why so many love it. Beauty can be found anywhere.

From *More Readers Theatre for Beginning Readers* by Suzanne I. Barchers and Charla R. Pfeffinger. Westport, CT: Libraries Unlimited/Teacher Ideas Press. Copyright © 2006.

The Three Brothers

Summary: This Polish folktale is about a wicked witch who would turn herself into a hawk and harass a town by breaking out the windows of the buildings. Three brothers try to kill the hawk. When the youngest one tries, he ends up in a land below the ground. There he finds Sara, who is being held prisoner. He also finds out how cruel his brothers really are.

Readability: 1.5

Staging: There are four staging areas for this play, with Leo moving among them. The first area, on the left, is for the brothers when they are all together. Leo should move to the right of the stage when he shoots the hawk. Leo should move to the center of the stage where he meets Sara and her sisters. He should move to the right when he meets the magician and back to his brothers, along with Sara, when he returns home.

Props: A sword, a stuffed snake, a bow and arrow

Characters:

Narrator One

Narrator Two

Al

Ed

Leo

Sara

Linda

Maggy

Magician

The Three Brothers

Narrator One: There once lived a wicked witch. She could turn herself into the shape of a hawk. She did this at night. She would fly into a small town. Here she would break the windows of the buildings. This upset all the people in the town.

Narrator Two: Al, Ed, and Leo were brothers who lived in the town. They decided to get rid of the hawk. Al and Ed tried to catch the hawk. But they failed. They went to see their younger brother.

Al: Leo, we have tried to get that hawk. As soon as it appears, we fall sleep.

Ed: We wake up when we hear the windows break. Then the hawk flies away. We think you may have better luck then we have had. You are much younger. Maybe you won't fall asleep.

Leo: The witch must be casting a spell on you. I will need to think of a way to stay awake. [*pause*] I know! I will take some rosebush thorns with me.

Al: How are thorns going to keep you awake, Leo?

Leo: I will put them under my chin. When my head falls forward, they will prick me. That will wake me.

Ed: That could work. Good luck.

Narrator One: That night Leo went to the church. There was a full moon in the sky. The night was as light as day. Leo sat for a while. Then he heard a fearful noise. He felt like he was going to fall asleep.

Narrator Two: Leo's head fell forward. The thorns pierced him. They hurt so much that he awoke at once. He saw the hawk.

Leo: You are not going to break any more windows in this town!

Narrator One: Leo lifted his bow and arrow. He shot at the hawk. The hawk fell near a big stone. Leo had wounded its right wing.

Narrator Two: He ran to find the hawk. Instead he saw a huge hole below the stone. He ran to get his brothers

Leo: Come quickly! You must help me.

Al: Have you killed the hawk?

Leo: I am not sure. It could just be hurt.

Ed: Why do you need our help?

Leo: There is a big hole where the hawk fell. I want you to lower me into the hole. Maybe I will find the hawk there.

Al: How can we lower you?

From *More Readers Theatre for Beginning Readers* by Suzanne I. Barchers and Charla R. Pfeffinger. Westport, CT: Libraries Unlimited/Teacher Ideas Press. Copyright © 2006.

Leo: Tie some rope around me. Then let me down the side of the hole. I will also need a light so I can see.

Narrator One: It was quite dark as Leo's brothers dropped him into the hole. When Leo reached the bottom, he couldn't believe what he saw!

Leo: What a lovely meadow! This is the most beautiful place I have ever seen. There is a whole world here.

Narrator Two: As he walked, he saw a huge stone castle. It had an iron gate in front of it. The gate was open. Leo entered the castle.

Leo: Is anyone here?

Narrator One: Leo went into a room where everything was made of copper. Sitting in the room was a lovely girl.

Sara: Who are you?

Leo: I'm Leo. Who are you?

Sara: I'm Sara. What are you doing here?

Leo: I shot a hawk. When it fell to the ground a large hole opened. I came down to see what was here. Do you live here alone?

Sara: No, my two sisters live here.

Leo: You are the most beautiful girl I have ever seen.

Sara: Why, thank you.

Leo: Would you come for a walk with me? I would like to get to know you.

Sara: I can never leave here.

Leo: Never?

Sara: Not as long as the witch is alive. If only you could kill her.

Leo: I could try. But I would need a better weapon.

Sara: She can be killed with a sword that is in my sister's room. It is so heavy no one has even been able to lift it.

Leo: Where is your sister's room?

Sara: In the silver room. My sister is there. She can show you the sword. If you cannot lift it, maybe my other sister can help you.

Narrator Two: Leo soon found the silver room. Linda was in the room.

Leo: Hello. Sara told me I could find a sword here.

Linda: You think you can lift it?

Leo: I want to try.

From *More Readers Theatre for Beginning Readers* by Suzanne I. Barchers and Charla R. Pfeffinger.
Westport, CT: Libraries Unlimited/Teacher Ideas Press. Copyright © 2006.

Linda: Well, there it is.

Narrator One: Leo tried to lift up the sword. It was too heavy. He dropped it. The other sister heard the sword drop. She came into the room.

Maggy: Who are you?

Leo: I am Leo. Sara hopes I can free her from the witch's spell.

Maggy: Why should you do that?

Leo: I want to be her friend.

Maggy: Then drink this.

Narrator One: Maggie handed Leo a magic brew. He drank one drop. He still could not lift the sword.

Maggy: You must drink two more drops for the brew to work.

Narrator Two: He drank three drops. Then he could lift the sword. He took the sword and hid in the castle. He waited for the old witch to come home.

Narrator One: A hawk swooped down upon a big apple tree. She shook some golden apples from the tree. They landed on the ground.

Narrator Two: The hawk flew to the ground. She changed from a hawk into a woman. Leo was waiting for this. He swung the sword with all his strength. She died with one blow.

Leo: Sara, I have freed you from the spell. Are you ready to leave with me?

Sara: How will we get back to your town? We are far below the ground.

Leo: My brothers are waiting at the top of the hole for me. They will pull us both up with the rope.

Sara: I want to take the treasure from our castle. We can put it in the chests. And my sisters must come along.

Leo: Fine. I will pack the chests. My brothers will pull them out of the hole. You and your sisters can go up ahead of me.

Narrator One: When the chests and sisters were pulled out, it was Leo's turn. He was not sure he could trust his brothers. He fastened a heavy stone on to the rope.

Narrator Two: The brothers pulled the stone halfway up and then let it drop. It fell and broke into a hundred pieces.

Leo: I knew I couldn't trust them. Now I am alone. And Sara is with my brothers!

Narrator One: Leo tried to make a life below the ground. One day he met a magician. The magician asked him why he was so sad. Leo told him why.

Magician: I think I can help you.

From *More Readers Theatre for Beginning Readers* by Suzanne I. Barchers and Charla R. Pfeffinger.
Westport, CT: Libraries Unlimited/Teacher Ideas Press. Copyright © 2006.

Leo: How?

Magician: I can fly you out of here. But first you must do something for me.

Leo: What?

Magician: Someone is trying to steal my children. I have hidden them in the golden apple tree. Hide near there. At midnight you will see my enemy. Kill him, and I will help you.

Leo: Why don't you save your children?

Magician: This enemy is too strong for me.

Leo: I'll try.

Narrator Two: Leo climbed up the tree. At midnight the wind began to blow. He heard a sound at the foot of the tree. He looked down and saw a snake creeping up the tree. It came higher and higher.

Narrator One: It stretched its huge head among the branches. Its eyes searched for the children. The children shook with fear. Leo swung his sword. With one blow, he stopped the snake forever. Soon the magician arrived.

Magician: Leo, you have saved my children! Climb on my back. I will fly you out of here.

Narrator Two: Soon Leo was home. He hurried to find his brothers. He burst into their home. They were sitting at the dinner table.

Sara: Leo, finally you are here!

Al: How did you get out of that hole? We thought you were dead.

Leo: I knew I couldn't trust you. I tied a stone on the rope.

Ed: Please, forgive us, Leo. We were wrong to try to kill you. You won't kill us, will you?

Leo: You are fools and dishonest. But I am not here to hurt you. I just want what is mine.

Al: Take whatever you want.

Leo: I want a third of the treasure. And I want Sara.

Sara: You saved our lives! You should have all the treasure.

Leo: No, Sara. I am not going to be greedy. There is enough for all of us.

Narrator One: Leo and Sara left. They became best friends. And one day they married. And of course they lived happily ever after.

From *More Readers Theatre for Beginning Readers* by Suzanne I. Barchers and Charla R. Pfeffinger. Westport, CT: Libraries Unlimited/Teacher Ideas Press. Copyright © 2006.

King Frost

Summary: This Russian fairy tale is about King Frost and a selfish stepmother. She forces Henry, her husband, to abandon his daughter, Sandy, in a frozen field. King Frost finds Sandy, rewarding her kindness with a rich robe and a chest of gold. Wanting to have her daughter receive the same wealth, the stepmother has Henry take her daughter to the same place in the frozen field. Her daughter freezes to death because of her selfish nature.

Readability: 1.7

Staging: Narrator One, Ruby, and the bird should stand on the left side of the stage, representing the farmer's home. Narrator Two and King Frost should stand on the right side of the stage, representing outside in the frozen field. Henry, Sandy, and Helen should move across the stage between the home and field at the appropriate times.

Props: Set up table and chairs for the kitchen in the home. Have plants or a drawing of trees to represent the frozen field.

Presentation: Voice inflection should follow the wording of the script. There is rhyme with the bird's part. If preferred, the audience can read this part. Write the words on cue cards and have Narrator Three hold them up at the appropriate time.

Characters:

Narrator One

Narrator Two

Narrator Three (nonspeaking, optional)

Ruby

Henry

Sandy

King Frost

Bird (optional audience part)

Helen

King Frost

Narrator One: Once upon a time there was a farmer named Henry. His wife had died. He became friends with a woman named Ruby. She had lost her husband some years before. They each had a daughter. They decided to marry. They would raise their daughters together.

Narrator Two: Ruby's daughter, Helen, was spoiled. She always got her own way. Henry's daughter, Sandy, was kind and good. Yet Ruby and Helen hated her. They blamed her for everything that went wrong. Sandy often would cry because of how they treated her. Ruby wanted to get Sandy out of their lives.

Ruby: Husband, I want you to send that daughter of yours away!

Henry: Why? What has she done to upset you so?

Ruby: I can't stand the sight of her. She cries day and night. It hurts my ears!

Henry: Where can I send her? I have no other family.

Ruby: I don't care where she goes. For all I care you can send her out into the field.

Henry: She will freeze to death.

Ruby: I don't care. Just get rid of her.

Narrator One: Henry begged Ruby to change her mind. She would not. She made him so unhappy that he finally gave in. He put Sandy in their sled. He took her to an open field. He kissed her and told her she could not come home. Then he left her to freeze to death.

Narrator Two: Sandy sat under a tree at the edge of the forest. She began to weep. Then she heard a sound.

Sandy: Who is there?

King Frost: I am King Frost, king of the red noses. Who are you?

Sandy: I am Sandy. Have you come to save me?

King Frost: Maybe. Answer this question. Are you warm?

Narrator One: Sandy was sure this was a trick question. She did not want to upset King Frost. She gave him the answer she thought he wanted to hear.

Sandy: Quite warm, King Frost.

Narrator Two: King Frost stooped down and bent over her. He did not believe her.

King Frost: Are you sure you are warm, beautiful girl?

Sandy: Oh, yes. I am quite warm, King Frost.

Narrator One: King Frost frowned. His eyes shone. He cracked his fingers. The crackling sound was very loud. The air seemed to get colder the more he cracked his fingers.

From *More Readers Theatre for Beginning Readers* by Suzanne I. Barchers and Charla R. Pfeffinger. Westport, CT: Libraries Unlimited/Teacher Ideas Press. Copyright © 2006.

King Frost: Are you still warm?

Narrator Two: Sandy was afraid to say she was cold. Once again, she told him that she was warm. King Frost was amazed! He knew she had to be freezing. He picked her up and took her to his sled. He wrapped her in the furs he kept there. When she had warmed up, he got a huge chest. Beautiful jewels and a rich robe were inside. The robe was sewn with gold and silver thread.

King Frost: Put on this robe. Are you warm now?

Sandy: Oh, yes, King Frost. I am very warm now.

Narrator One: King Frost put Sandy in his sled. He drove away.

Sandy: Where are you taking me?

King Frost: I am taking you to your home.

Sandy: But they do not want me.

King Frost: Oh, I think this robe and chest will change that.

Sandy: Why are you doing this for me?

King Frost: Because you are sweet and good. You should be rewarded for having a kind heart.

Narrator Two: Meanwhile, Ruby wanted to be sure that Sandy was dead.

Ruby: Henry, you had better go get Sandy's body. We need to bury her.

Narrator One: Just as Henry started through the door, their bird began to talk.

Bird/Narrator Three: Awrk. Awrk. Sandy will have much silver and gold. But Helen will freeze quite stiff and cold.

Henry: What did he say?

Ruby: Nothing. He's just a foolish bird! Bird, I am sure you meant to say *Helen* shall have much silver and gold. *Sandy* will freeze quite stiff and cold.

Bird/Narrator Three: Awrk. Awrk. No, you are wrong. Sandy will have much silver and gold. But Helen will freeze quite stiff and cold.

Narrator Two: Ruby wouldn't believe the bird. She tried to get it to stop talking, but it wouldn't. The bird always said the same words. Suddenly the door flew open.

Narrator One: Sandy pushed a great chest into the house. Her robe glittered with silver and gold. Ruby's eyes got big.

Narrator Two: Henry was very happy to see his daughter alive. He asked her about the robe and chest. She told him about King Frost and his kindness. Of course, Ruby wanted Helen to have the same.

Ruby: Henry, take Helen to the same field where you took Sandy. Leave her on the same exact spot!

Henry: Why? Sandy has brought enough riches for all of us.

Ruby: I want Helen to have her own riches.

Narrator One: Henry took Helen into the field. He left her beneath the same tree. Soon King Frost came by. He saw Helen sitting on the cold ground.

King Frost: Who are you?

Helen: I am Helen. Have you come to give me a robe to keep me warm?

King Frost: Why, are you cold?

Helen: What a stupid question. You must be a blind old fool! Can't you see that my hands and feet are nearly frozen?

Narrator Two: King Frost walked back and forth. He asked her again and again if she were cold. Each time she answered rudely. She kept asking for a warm robe and a chest of jewels. He got very angry. He knew she was selfish and greedy. He got in his sled and left.

Narrator One: Ruby waited for Helen to return. Finally, she began to worry about her.

Ruby: Henry, get out the sled and horses. Go to the field and find Helen. Bring her home. I am sure she has met King Frost by now. I wonder why he didn't bring her back.

Bird/Narrator Three: Awrk. Awrk. Helen is frozen quite stiff and cold. She shall never have a chest full of gold.

Ruby: Don't say such wicked things about Helen. You should say she will marry a mighty king. Perhaps it will be King Frost himself. Henry, hurry and get Helen. Don't forget the chest.

Narrator One: When Ruby heard the sled return, she rushed out to meet her daughter. As the bird said, Helen was stiff and cold.

Narrator Two: Ruby took her Helen's body in her arms. As Ruby held her frozen daughter, she also became chilled. She caught a cold and died within a month.

Narrator One: And Sandy, Henry, and the bird lived happily for many years.

From *More Readers Theatre for Beginning Readers* by Suzanne I. Barchers and Charla R. Pfeffinger. Westport, CT: Libraries Unlimited/Teacher Ideas Press. Copyright © 2006.

The Lute Player

Summary: This is a Russian folktale about a king who gets so bored that he leaves his wife to go on an adventure, only to end up in prison. When he sends his wife instructions on how to save him, she disguises herself as a boy and travels to find him. Using her lute to lure King Conrad's attention, she frees her husband as a reward for her soothing music.

Readability: 1.7

Staging: The narrators should sit on left side of the staging area with the other readers sitting in a semicircle on the right side.

Props: None.

Presentation: Voice inflection should reflect the script.

Characters:

Narrator One

Narrator Two

King

Queen

Guard

Maid

King Conrad

Minister

The Lute Player

Narrator One: Once upon a time there lived a king and queen. They were very happy. They had nothing to worry about. They also had nothing to do. The king grew bored. He decided to take his army and go out into the world.

King: My dear, I don't know how long I will be gone. Please take care of yourself while I am away.

Queen: Do you have to leave? We have such a good life.

King: I know, but I am bored. I need a good adventure.

Queen: Why are you taking so many soldiers? Do you expect to get into a fight along the way?

King: You never know, dear. It is always better to be ready. If there is a fight, I shall win.

Narrator Two: The king and his men got on a ship. They went to a far away country. They started marching to the home of that country's king.

Narrator One: They had many fights on the way. They won each fight. Then they came to a mountain pass. A large army met them. There was a short fight. The king's army lost. He was taken prisoner.

Guard: At night, you will stay chained up with the rest of the men.

King: But I am a king!

Guard: I don't care who you are. Now I am in charge. In the morning, you will help plow the fields.

King: Plow the fields! This is no way to treat a king.

Narrator Two: No one would listen to him. Each night he was chained to the wall. Each morning he had to plow the fields. He had to work with another prisoner. They were just like oxen. When it was dark, the men would go back to the prison.

Narrator One: It was three years before the king could send his wife a letter.

Queen: Oh, at last! The king has sent me a letter.

Maid: What does it say?

Queen: He wants me to sell all that we own. Then I am to use the money to free him from prison. I have to go there now.

Maid: But that is not safe! It isn't safe for you to go alone.

Queen: I know what to do. I will cut off my hair and dress as a boy.

Maid: Are you sure that you want to do that?

Queen: Yes, I am. And I will take my lute to play as I look for the king.

Maid: Please do not do this. There must be a better way.

From *More Readers Theatre for Beginning Readers* by Suzanne I. Barchers and Charla R. Pfeffinger. Westport, CT: Libraries Unlimited/Teacher Ideas Press. Copyright © 2006.

Narrator Two: But the queen would not change her mind. She dressed up like a boy. Then she began her search for the king. After a long walk, she came to a palace. She walked all around it.

Narrator One: At the back, she saw the prison. She went into the great court in front of the palace. Then she began to play her lute. The music was so lovely. All the people stopped to listen. Then she began to sing. Her voice was so sweet. As soon as the song was done, the king had her come to see him.

King Conrad: Welcome to my home. Where are you from?

Queen: I live far away, from across the sea.

King Conrad: Why are you here?

Queen: I love to travel. I earn my living by playing my lute.

King Conrad: Stay and play for a few days. I'll let you go when you want. Then I'll give you what you wish.

Queen: I'll be happy to stay and play for you.

King Conrad: Thank you. Your music makes me happy.

Narrator Two: After three days, she was ready to leave.

Queen: It is time for me to leave, my king.

King Conrad: I promised you a reward. What do you want?

Queen: I would like one of your prisoners.

King Conrad: Why would you want one of them?

Queen: To keep me company on my way home. And he will always remind me of you and your kindness.

King Conrad: Come then and make your choice.

Narrator One: The king took the lute player to the prison. She walked until she found her husband.

Queen: I will take that one.

King Conrad: Are you sure? He is quite old and looks very weak.

Queen: Yes, I am sure. I want that man.

Narrator Two: The queen was still dressed as a lute player. Her husband did not know who she was. Soon they were near their home.

King: Please, let me go now, young man. I am no common prisoner. I am the king of this country. Let me go. You may have all you want as a reward.

Queen: I don't want a reward for freeing you. If you must leave, then go in peace.

King: Why don't you come with me? Be my guest at the palace.

Queen: I may come to see you later. But now I must be on my way.

King: Good-bye then and thank you.

Narrator One: The queen took a shortcut to their home. She got there before the king did. She changed into a dress and waited for him. When he got home, he did not go to see her. Instead, he met with his council.

King: What sort of wife do I have? Before I left, she loved me and was kind. Did she help me when I was in prison?

Minister: Sir. She went away. We could not find her. No one knew where she went. She just got back today.

King: I don't want to hear any more. I want you to question her.

Minister: But Sir. She is our queen. How can we question her?

King: That is not my problem. You don't seem to understand. If it had not been for a young lute player, I would still be in prison. Because of him, I was let go. It was his reward for his fine lute playing.

Narrator Two: The queen's maid heard the king talking. She went to tell the queen her life was in danger. The queen put the boys clothing back on. She got her lute. Then she slipped into the court in front of the palace. She began to play and sing.

King: Listen. Do you hear that? It is the lute player I was telling you about. Come with me.

Narrator One: They all went to the court.

King: I am so glad to see you. Let me give you a reward.

Queen: I am sure you will be as kind as King Conrad.

King: Of course. I owe you my life.

Queen: Then I want … you.

King: Me? But—

Narrator Two: The king was stunned as the young man threw off his disguise. There stood the queen. They were all glad to see her. Finally, the king and the queen were home.

Narrator One: And now that they were home, they had nothing to worry about. They only needed to do one thing—to live happily ever after.

Clever Maria

Summary: In this story from Portugal, a king sends a merchant on an errand. When he returns, he finds his youngest daughter, Maria, missing and his eldest daughters married. Maria has upset the king, and he wants revenge. He demands that the merchant bring Maria to him. Maria outwits the king in the end.

Readability: 1.8

Staging: The narrators should sit on left side of the staging area. The king should sit on a high stool. The other readers should sit in a semicircle around the king.

Props: None.

Presentation: Maria should sound sweet. The merchant mostly should sound desperate. The king should sound imperious.

Characters:

Narrator One

Narrator Two

Merchant

Leola

Bertha

Maria

King

Old Woman

Gardener

Page

Clever Maria

Narrator One: A merchant lived next to a royal palace. He had three daughters. Their names were Maria, Leola, and Bertha. They were all pretty. Maria was the youngest. She was the prettiest of the three.

Narrator Two: One day the king sent for the merchant. The king wanted him to go on an errand. The merchant did not want to go. He did not like leaving his daughters at home alone.

Merchant: The king is sending me on an errand for him. I will be gone for some time.

Leola: Do you have to go?

Merchant: I fear I must go. When the king gives an order, you have no choice. You must not let anyone into the house while I am gone.

Bertha: We will be fine. You don't need to worry, father.

Merchant: Just the same, I am leaving each one of you a pot of basil. These pots are magical. When I come back, they will tell me what has been going on.

Narrator One: The merchant left. The next day the king and his two friends came to visit the three girls. They were just sitting down to supper.

Leola: Won't you join us for supper?

King: No, we'll just sit here while you finish.

Maria: That will never do. We will get you something cool to drink. We will be right back. It is in the cellar.

King: Why must you all go?

Maria: Well, I have the key to open the door, but I need my Leola to hold the light so I can see. Then we will need someone to carry the bottles.

King: No, do not bother. We are not thirsty.

Leola: Very well.

Maria: No, that would be rude. You can all stay here. I will go by myself.

Narrator Two: Maria left the room and went to the hall. At the end of the hall, she set down the light. She slipped out the back door. Then she ran to a neighbor's house. She knocked at the door.

Old Woman: Who is out there so late at night?

Maria: Oh, please let me in. I am afraid to be at home. May I stay here with you tonight?

Old Woman: Where is your father?

Maria: The king sent him on an errand. We are there alone.

From *More Readers Theatre for Beginning Readers* by Suzanne I. Barchers and Charla R. Pfeffinger. Westport, CT: Libraries Unlimited/Teacher Ideas Press. Copyright © 2006.

Old Woman: Then come in and stay.

Narrator One: The next day Maria went home. Her sisters' pots of basil had wilted. They had not obeyed their father.

Narrator Two: The king had pear trees in his garden. One tree grew next to Leola's window.

Leola: Maria, I want some pears from the king's garden.

Maria: Those are the king's pears!

Leola: You can get into the garden. Go down this rope. Then once you have picked the pears, tie the rope under your arms. I will pull you up.

Maria: All right.

Narrator One: Maria let herself into the garden by the rope. She picked some pears. She began to tie the rope under her arms. Her sister called down to her.

Leola: Oh, look! There are some lemons on the tree over there. Would you get one or two of them?

Maria: Is there anything else you want?

Narrator Two: Maria turned around to pick the lemons. There was the gardener. He took her by the arm.

Gardener: What are you doing here? You are a little thief.

Maria: Don't call me names! Let me go.

Gardener: No, I am taking you to the king. No one steals fruit from his garden while I am in charge.

Narrator One: Maria did not want to see the king. She gave the gardener a big push. He fell into the bushes. Maria grabbed the rope. She climbed back up to the window.

Narrator Two: The next day, Bertha wanted some oranges from the garden.

Bertha: Maria, please go into garden and bring me some oranges.

Maria: No. I am not going back there again.

Bertha: But Maria, I really want some oranges. I will wait right here to pull you up on the rope.

Narrator One: At last she gave in. She went down the rope into the king's garden. This time she met the king!

King: Ah, here you are again. You are trying to steal the fruit from my garden. This time you will pay for your misdeeds. Come with me to the palace. There you shall pay the fine for stealing.

From *More Readers Theatre for Beginning Readers* by Suzanne I. Barchers and Charla R. Pfeffinger. Westport, CT: Libraries Unlimited/Teacher Ideas Press. Copyright © 2006.

Narrator Two: They walked back toward the house. At times, the king would look behind at Maria. He wanted to make sure she had not run away. All of a sudden, he turned around. She was gone! He could not find her. The king ordered a search in the town. There was no sign of Maria. This made the king so mad that he became quite sick. For months his family feared he would die.

Narrator One: Maria had run away. Finally the merchant came home. He could see that his daughters had not obeyed him. Two of the basil plants were wilted. And Maria was gone. He was very sad.

Narrator Two: Years passed. The other two sisters got married. Leola had two babies. One day Maria secretly slipped to Leola's house. She put the two babies into a basket. She covered them with flowers. No one could see them. Then she dressed herself as a boy. She put the basket on her head. She walked slowly past the palace. She called out to all who could hear her.

Maria: Who will take these flowers to the king?

King: Page, do you hear that? I know that voice. It is Maria. Quick, go outside. Bring me those flowers and Maria.

Narrator One: When the page got there, Maria was gone. The basket was still there. The page brought it to the king. He looked under the flowers. He saw the babies. He was mad at Maria.

King: I can't believe she got away. It is time her father pays for her misdeeds.

Narrator Two: The king sent a message to the merchant. The king told him to bring him a coat made of stone. The poor merchant! He missed Maria so much. And now the king expected him to make a coat of stone. He knew the king would be the ruin of him. Then Maria came in the door.

Merchant: Maria! I am so glad to see you! I have missed you so much!

Maria: I have missed you too, Father.

Merchant: I don't know what to do, my dear. I have such troubles. The king wants me to make a coat of stone for him. Now, how am I going to do that?

Maria: Don't worry about making a coat of stone. Take this bit of chalk and go to the palace. Say you have come to measure the king.

Merchant: Why should I do that?

Maria: Trust me. Just go measure the king for his coat.

Narrator One: The merchant took the chalk. He went to see the king.

King: Why are you here?

Merchant: I have come to measure you for your coat.

King: I don't want you to measure me for a coat.

Merchant: I can't make a stone coat if I don't measure you.

King: Why don't you just bring me your daughter? That would be much easier.

Narrator Two: The merchant went home. He spoke to Maria.

Merchant: The king would not let me measure him. He wants you, not a coat.

Maria: I know what to do. Have a doll made that looks just like me. Attach a string to its head. The head should nod "Yes" or "No" when the string is pulled.

Merchant: I don't see how this will make the king happy.

Maria: Just trust me, Father.

Narrator One: The merchant got the doll made. Meanwhile, the king waited in his palace. He was sure the merchant would bring Maria to the palace. He told his page what to do.

King: The merchant will come with his daughter. Put her in my room. Make sure she stays there.

Page: What should I do with her father?

King: Send him home.

Narrator Two: The next day, the merchant and Maria came to the palace. Maria had hidden the doll under her coat. The page put Maria in the king's room. She put the doll on the couch and hid behind the couch. She held on to the string that was fastened to the doll's head. Soon the king came in the room.

King: Maria, I hope you are well.

Narrator One: The king saw the doll nod. He walked around. He didn't see that the doll was not Maria.

King: Now we have some things to talk about. First, you stole the fruit from my garden. Next, you ran away from me. And you left your sister's babies here.

Narrator Two: Each time the king spoke, the doll's head would nod. The king became mad. He wanted Maria to answer him. He drew his sword out. He cut off the doll's head. It fell toward him. He realized what he had done. He was so sorry.

King: Ah, Maria. You never knew me. I loved you so much. I wish this had not happened.

Narrator One: Maria was shocked by his words. She jumped up. She threw herself into his arms.

Narrator Two: Maria and the king spent many hours talking. Before long, they were married. They lived happily for many years.

The Enchanted Prince

Summary: In this tale from Poland, a princess befriends an injured crow that is really a prince. She gives three years of her life to help him endure and then break the spell that was cast on him. Although this story ends with the usual living happily ever after, the script emphasizes the importance of keeping a promise.

Readability: 1.8

Staging: The narrators should sit on the left of the stage. The three readers should sit on the right.

Props: The stage can have a backdrop showing a castle in ruins.

Presentation: Voice inflection should reflect the script.

Characters:

> Narrator One
>
> Narrator Two
>
> Crow
>
> Allie
>
> Katie

The Enchanted Prince

Narrator One: Three young princesses lived in a palace. Close to the palace was a castle. No one lived there. The garden still grew. It was full of blooming flowers. Allie was the youngest princess. She often walked in the garden.

Narrator Two: Allie walked under the lime trees. A black crow hopped out of a rosebush in front of her. The bird was hurt and bleeding. Allie was upset when she saw the poor crow.

Allie: Oh, you poor crow. You are hurt!

Crow: I am not really a black crow. I am a prince. A witch put me under a spell. I must be a crow for seven years.

Allie: Oh, dear! That is sad!

Crow: That's not all. The witch torments me day and night.

Allie: Is there any way I can help you?

Crow: There is only one way that you can help. You would have to leave your family. And you would have to live in this ruined castle.

Allie: I can't live in this mess! It's dirty and run down.

Crow: There is one room in the castle with a golden bed in it. It would be yours.

Allie: So to help you, I have to sleep on a golden bed. And I could not see my family?

Crow: Well, there is one more thing.

Allie: Just one?

Crow: Yes and it will be the hardest. During the night, you may see strange things. And you may hear strange sounds. You cannot scream or make a sound.

Allie: Why?

Crow: The witch will be even meaner to me.

Allie: I do hate to see you suffer so much. [*pause*] Okay, I will do as you ask.

Crow: Thank you. I promise it won't be for forever.

Narrator One: Allie took a few of her things. She moved into the room with the golden bed. That night she lay down on the golden bed. She was very tired, but she could not sleep. At midnight, she heard things coming down the hall. Then something banged on her door. She would not open it. The door flew open. Strange creatures entered the room.

Narrator Two: They lit a fire in the huge fireplace. They put a large pot of water in it. The water started to boil. The creatures came toward the bed. Allie was so scared. But she didn't make a sound. All of sudden a crow appeared. The creatures went away.

From *More Readers Theatre for Beginning Readers* by Suzanne I. Barchers and Charla R. Pfeffinger.
Westport, CT: Libraries Unlimited/Teacher Ideas Press. Copyright © 2006.

Allie: Oh, thank you! You scared them away!

Crow: No, thank you for staying quiet. I know you must have been scared. Staying quiet kept things from getting worse.

Allie: You're welcome, I think. This was so scary. Is it going to be like this every night?

Crow: I am afraid so. Will you stay here anyway?

Allie: Of course. I promised I would, didn't I? At least I know what to expect.

Narrator One: Allie's older sister, Katie, wondered where Allie was. She looked for her. She finally found Allie in the castle.

Katie: Allie, why are you living in this terrible place. And why are you all by yourself?

Allie: I am helping a young prince endure an evil spell.

Katie: Aren't you lonely out here?

Allie: No, I like the peace and quiet.

Katie: This castle is in ruins.

Allie: Not in my bedroom. I'll show it to you.

Narrator Two: Allie showed Katie the bedroom.

Katie: Oh, this is beautiful. Let me stay the night with you.

Allie: I don't think that is a good idea, Katie.

Katie: Why not?

Allie: Strange things happen here in the night. I am not sure you want to be here.

Katie: Please let me stay.

Allie: If you want to. But if you get scared, just remember that I warned you.

Katie: If you can stand being here with the strange things going on, then I can, too. After all, I am older than you are!

Narrator One: At midnight the creatures appeared. Katie screamed with fear. She left and never came back. Allie stayed, living alone during the day. Each night the creatures came to visit. Each morning the crow came and thanked her for help. He told her his pains were less each day. Two years passed. The crow asked Allie for more help.

Crow: In one more year, I can be free. My seven years will be done. Before I can become human, I need you to do one more thing for me.

Allie: What is that?

Crow: You must leave the castle.

Allie: That's all?

From *More Readers Theatre for Beginning Readers* by Suzanne I. Barchers and Charla R. Pfeffinger. Westport, CT: Libraries Unlimited/Teacher Ideas Press. Copyright © 2006.

Crow: No, you have to become someone's maid.

Allie: And then you will be free?

Crow: Yes. I know I am asking a lot of you.

Allie: No, that's fine. I promised to help you free yourself from the spell. I have kept that promise. I will go find work as a maid.

Crow: Thank you. When the year is up, I will come and get you. That is a promise I'm making to you.

Narrator Two: For one year, Allie worked as a maid. The work was hard. She was treated poorly.

Narrator One: One evening she was spinning flax. She heard a rustling beside her. She saw a handsome young man. He knelt down and kissed her hands.

Crow: I am the prince you have been helping. I am free. As I promised, I have come for you. I want to marry you. We will live in my castle.

Allie: But your castle is in ruins!

Crow: No, my dear. It has been rebuilt. It is a fine castle.

Narrator Two: Allie and the prince kept their promises. Allie chose to marry him. They lived happily ever after.

From *More Readers Theatre for Beginning Readers* by Suzanne I. Barchers and Charla R. Pfeffinger. Westport, CT: Libraries Unlimited/Teacher Ideas Press. Copyright © 2006.

The Hazelnut Child

Summary: This German tale is about a couple who wants a child, even if the child is only the size of a hazelnut—and that is just what they get. But little Fritz does not let his size stop him from finding a way to provide for himself and his parents.

Readability: 1.8

Staging: Have the narrators sit on low stools on the left side of the stage. The three neighbors can walk slowly across the stage, turned toward the audience, as they read their lines. Mother and Father can stand in the center of the stage. Fritz should sit on a high stool between them.

Props: Have students create a mural with hazelnut trees in the background.

Characters:

Narrator One

Narrator Two

Neighbor One

Neighbor Two

Neighbor Three

Mother

Fritz

Father

The Hazelnut Child

Narrator One: There was once a man and wife. They had no children. They wanted a child so much. They did not care if he was big or little.

Narrator Two: Finally, they had a son. He was very little. In fact, he was exactly the size of a hazelnut. He never grew an inch taller.

Narrator One: They named him Fritz. He was very smart. Their neighbors talked about him once he was old enough to play outside.

Neighbor One: Have you ever met Fritz?

Neighbor Two: Yes. He is so little!

Neighbor Three: Yes, he is. But he is a smart little boy.

Neighbor One: He can already read!

Neighbor Three: He is kind, too. He helped me find my cat. He knew just where to look.

Neighbor Two: Many years went by. One day Fritz and his mother talked about his future.

Mother: Fritz, you are fifteen years old now. What are you going to do with your life?

Fritz: I am going to be a messenger.

Mother: What a foolish idea! You a messenger! Your feet are so little! You can't walk fast enough.

Fritz: Mother, I am going to be a messenger! Why don't you send me on an errand? You'll see how fast I can return.

Mother: Very well. Go to your Aunt Jane's and fetch me a comb.

Narrator One: Fritz jumped up and ran into the street. He found a man on horseback. He was riding to the same village his aunt lived. Fritz crept up the horse's leg and sat down under the saddle. He began to pinch the horse's back. This caused the horse to rear up and gallop away.

Narrator Two: When they reached the village, Fritz quit pinching the horse. The tired horse slowed down. Fritz crept down the horse's leg. He ran to his aunt's home. He asked her for a comb.

Narrator One: As he started home he found a rider going back to his village. He crept up the horse's leg. He sat down under the saddle. He began to pinch the horse's back. Soon he was home.

Fritz: Here is the comb you wanted, Mother.

Mother: But how did you manage to do this so quickly?

Fritz: That is my secret, Mother. I don't need to be big. I just need to be smart. I said being a messenger was a good job for me. I was right.

From *More Readers Theatre for Beginning Readers* by Suzanne I. Barchers and Charla R. Pfeffinger.
Westport, CT: Libraries Unlimited/Teacher Ideas Press. Copyright © 2006.

Mother: Yes, you were.

Narrator Two: Fritz used this same idea to help his father. Often his father would take his horse out into the fields to graze. One day Fritz went along.

Father: Fritz, I forgot something. I need to go back home. I want you to stay here. Look after the horse.

Fritz: OK, Father. The horse and I will be just fine.

Narrator Two: While his father was gone, a robber passed by. He saw the horse grazing in the field. The robber thought no one was watching for the horse. Fritz saw the robber coming. He climbed up the horse's tail.

Narrator One: The robber mounted the horse. Fritz began to pinch the horse on the back. This made the horse so mad that it galloped straight home. Fritz's father was amazed. There was a stranger riding his horse.

Father: What are you doing on my horse?

Robber: What do you mean? This is my horse.

Father: No, it is not! This is my horse. Look, here is my mark.

Robber: I found it in the field. No one was caring for it.

Narrator Two: Fritz climbed down from the horse.

Fritz: Father, this man stole your horse. I climbed up the tail and pinched it. That's why it came straight home. Are you going to get the sheriff?

Father: Yes! Good work, son! And you are so little!

Fritz: I don't need to be big. I just need to be smart.

Narrator One: Fritz turned twenty years old. He decided it was time to live on his own.

Fritz: Father and Mother, I am leaving home.

Mother: Where are you going?

Fritz: I am going out into the world to become rich.

Father: How do you expect to become rich? What can you do?

Fritz: I have a plan. I don't need to be big. I just need to be smart.

Mother: Father, I know Fritz will be fine. Fritz, just take care of yourself.

Fritz: I will, Mother. Good-bye.

Narrator Two: Fritz walked a long ways. That night he crept onto a roof. Some storks slept on the roof. He climbed on to the back of the father stork. Then he tied a silk rope round one of its wings. Next, Fritz lay down on the soft feathers. He fell asleep.

From *More Readers Theatre for Beginning Readers* by Suzanne I. Barchers and Charla R. Pfeffinger. Westport, CT: Libraries Unlimited/Teacher Ideas Press. Copyright © 2006.

Narrator One: The next morning, the storks flew south. Winter was coming. Fritz held on to the silk rope. They flew through the air until they reached a kingdom far away. When they landed, Fritz untied the cord. He jumped off the stork's back.

Narrator Two: When the people saw Fritz, they were amazed by his size. They took him to see the king. The king liked him. He grew so fond of Fritz that he gave him a diamond. It was four times as big as Fritz.

Narrator One: Soon it was time for the storks to fly back north. Fritz tied the diamond under the stork's neck with a ribbon. He tied his silk rope onto the stork. They flew back home. There, he untied the ribbon from the stork's neck. The diamond fell to the ground. Fritz hid it under sand and stones. Then he ran to get his parents.

Fritz: Father, Mother! Hurry! I have brought you great riches.

Father: What could you have brought? Anything you could carry would be small.

Fritz: Please come with me.

Mother: Okay, Fritz, we will come with you. But I don't understand.

Narrator Two: When Fritz dug up the diamond, his parents were stunned.

Father: Where did you get this diamond? It must be worth a small fortune.

Narrator One: Fritz told his parents about his trip.

Fritz: I told you I would find a way to take care of us forever.

Mother: You were right again, Fritz. You have proven it. You don't need to be big.

Father, Mother, and Fritz: You just need to be smart!

From *More Readers Theatre for Beginning Readers* by Suzanne I. Barchers and Charla R. Pfeffinger. Westport, CT: Libraries Unlimited/Teacher Ideas Press. Copyright © 2006.

Blockhead Hans

Summary: This lighthearted Dutch folktale is about Hans, considered a blockhead by his family and friends. When a princess seeks a husband, however, this blockhead wins her heart.

Readability: 1.9

Staging: The narrators should stand on the left side of the staging area. The father and brothers should begin their reading on the right side of the stage. As the brothers travel toward the palace, they should move toward the left of the stage. The princess should sit on the far left. As the brothers are dismissed they should exit the stage.

Props: Stuffed blackbird, bottom of a shoe, and some black goop to represent mud in a small container, book bags to represent saddlebags to hold the bird and shoe, and an oversized hankie or rag hanging from Hans's pocket.

Presentation: Dirk and Gerrit should sound arrogant. Hans should sound simple but kind. The princess should sound annoyed at first, then intrigued.

Characters:

Narrator One

Narrator Two

Dirk

Gerrit

Blockhead Hans

Father

Princess

Blockhead Hans

Narrator One: An old squire lived far out in the country. He had three sons. He was most fond of Dirk and Gerrit. They thought they knew a lot. If they only knew half that much! The old squire did not have much use for Hans. He thought he was quite dull. He called him Blockhead Hans.

Narrator Two: Now, the king had a daughter. It was time for her to marry. She announced that she wanted to talk with the men of the country. She would marry the man who knew best how to choose his words. The two brothers both wanted to marry her. They practiced things they would say to impress her.

Dirk: Gerrit, I am sure I shall win her hand! Look at all the Latin I know.

Gerrit: Don't count on it, Dirk. I know all the laws of business. I will be able to talk with her about those. I am sure this will be of use to the princess.

Dirk: I think I can impress her more with my ability to use Latin. And I know the last three years of the newspaper. I am sure that will be useful to her.

Gerrit: That's all you can do? Well, my drawings of roses and flowers are the best.

Dirk: You think that will win her? Well, we soon shall see, won't we?

Narrator One: Their father gave each of them a fine horse. They were ready to leave for the palace. Hans came home just as they were about to leave.

Blockhead Hans: Aha! Where are you two going? You have on your best clothes!

Gerrit: We are going to see the princess! She is looking for a husband. Don't tell me you don't know that.

Blockhead Hans: No I didn't know. That sounds grand! I will go with you! Maybe I will win her hand.

Narrator Two: The brothers laughed at him. Then they rode off. They would not wait for him. Hans tried to get help from his father.

Blockhead Hans: Sir, I must have a horse! I may want to marry her.

Father: You are a fool! I won't give you a horse. She wants a man who can speak well. That isn't you! Your brothers are smart. They have worked for a week to get ready.

Blockhead Hans: Very well, then. I will ride my goat to the palace.

Narrator One: And so he did. He sat on his goat. He hit his heels on its sides. He went rattling down the high road as fast as he could.

Blockhead Hans: Hop, hop, hop! Hop, hop, hop! Here I come, my princess!

Narrator Two: Hans shouted and sang as he went down the road. He was heard by all. Hans's brothers rode just a bit ahead of him. They rode quietly. They thought about all they were going to say when they met the princess. Soon Hans caught up with them.

Blockhead Hans: Wait for me a bit. Just look what I found on the road. It's a dead crow.

Gerrit: Hans! What are you going to do with it?

Blockhead Hans: With the crow? [*pause*] I shall give it to the princess!

Dirk: Ha, ha! She will love that! Come on Gerrit. Let's get going.

Narrator One: The brothers rode off, and Hans was left behind. It wasn't long before they heard him call again.

Blockhead Hans: Here I am again! Look at what I have just found! It isn't every day you find such a great thing on the side of the road.

Dirk: Hans! That is just the bottom half of an old shoe. Are you going to give that to the princess, too?

Blockhead Hans: Of course I shall! You never know when a find like this will come in handy.

Gerrit: What would she do with half a shoe? You can't wear it. Ha, ha, ha!

Narrator Two: Once again, the two brothers rode off. Before long Blockhead Hans caught up with them again.

Blockhead Hans: Wait up! Look at this find! This is the best yet.

Gerrit: What have you found now, Blockhead Hans?

Blockhead Hans: This will really please the princess.

Narrator One: Blockhead Hans put his hand in his pocket. Then he pulled out a small box. He pulled off the lid. Some mud was inside.

Dirk: Why, that's just mud, right from the ditch!

Blockhead Hans: Of course it is! It is the best kind! Look how it runs through my fingers!

Gerrit: Come on Dirk. We don't have time for this nonsense.

Narrator Two: The brothers rode quickly ahead of Blockhead Hans. Dust and sparks flew all around him. They reached the gate of the town an hour before he did. The men who wanted to marry the princess were lined up. They had numbers that showed the order in which they arrived. Then they were arranged in rows of six. They were packed into the outer court. They couldn't even move their arms.

Narrator One: All of the country's people were standing around the king's throne to see the princess greet each man. As each one came into the room, all of his fine phrases went out of his head! Each man seemed duller than the other one. The princess sent each one away.

From *More Readers Theatre for Beginning Readers* by Suzanne I. Barchers and Charla R. Pfeffinger. Westport, CT: Libraries Unlimited/Teacher Ideas Press. Copyright © 2006.

Princess: Away! Out with you!

Narrator Two: Finally, it was time for the brothers. They had become more and more nervous. Dirk knew the dictionary by heart when he left home. Now he couldn't remember one word! Gerrit became upset by the floor creaking below him. He couldn't remember one law!

Narrator One: That wasn't all. Three reporters and an old man were standing by the window. They were writing down everything that was being said. They were going to publish everything that was said by the winner in their paper the next day. Finally, it was Dirk's turn.

Dirk: Ahem! It is really hot in here, isn't it!

Princess: Of course it is! My father is roasting chickens today!

Narrator Two: Dirk stood there like a fool. He wanted to say something witty. Finally, the princess got tired of waiting.

Princess: Take him out! Who is next?

Gerrit: I am. My, how hot it is in here!

Princess: Of course! We are roasting chickens today!

Gerrit: How do you, um! How do you, um …

Princess: [*shaking her head*] Never mind. It doesn't matter! Take him out! Who's next?

Narrator One: Blockhead Hans came into the hall riding on his goat!

Blockhead Hans: I say! How roasting hot it is in here!

Princess: Of course it is! We are roasting chickens today!

Blockhead Hans: That sounds good! [*Takes crow from saddle bags.*] I found this crow along the way here. Can I roast it with the chickens?

Princess: A crow? Of course! But do you have anything you can put it in? I have no extra pots or pans.

Blockhead Hans: Oh yes, I do have something that I found along the road. I believe this can be used.

Narrator Two: He drew out the old shoe and put the crow in it.

Princess: How clever of you! With chicken and crow we shall have quite a meal. But we need to have some soup. Where shall we get it?

Blockhead Hans: I have that in my pocket! I have so much soup that I can throw some away!

Narrator One: He poured some mud out of the container and the princess began to laugh.

From *More Readers Theatre for Beginning Readers* by Suzanne I. Barchers and Charla R. Pfeffinger. Westport, CT: Libraries Unlimited/Teacher Ideas Press. Copyright © 2006.

Princess: I like you! You can answer questions, you can speak, and you are clever. I believe I will marry you. Come closer. [*whispering*] See those three reporters and that old editor standing by the window? Do you know that they have written down every word that we've said to put in the paper tomorrow? The older editor is the worst writer of all. He doesn't hear very well and always gets things all mixed up.

Narrator Two: She said this to tease Blockhead Hans. She wanted to see what he would do next.

Blockhead Hans: Ah! So the three young men are good writers?

Princess: Yes, it's just the old editor who is always misquoting me.

Blockhead Hans: Then I need to give the old editor my best comments.

Narrator One: He turned his pocket inside out and threw mud right into the old editor's face.

Princess: Ha! That was smart. I couldn't have thought of that.

Narrator Two: Blockhead Hans so impressed the princess that he got a wife and a crown. And one day he became king.

Narrator One: It's hard to believe, isn't it?

Narrator Two: Or can we believe it at all? The only proof we have is an article in the penny newspapers. It's all about an old editor getting mud on his face. Do you think he reported the truth?

Part 3

Second-Grade Scripts

The Glass Mountain

Summary: This Polish fairy tale is about a princess who is held captive at the top of a glass mountain. For seven years, she waits for someone to free her. When Pete finally makes it to the top, he isn't clever enough to find a way down the mountain. In the end, this script asks the students to find ways to get the princess and her treasures down the mountain.

Readability: 2.0

Staging: Readers should stand in their sections in small clusters as they read. The sections should be lined up as follows: Readers A, Readers C, Readers D, Readers B, Readers E. This will keep the readings more spontaneous in sound.

Props: None.

Presentation: Divide fifteen readers into five sections for this choral reading. Speakers should work on dramatic voice inflection.

Characters:

Readers A

Readers B

Readers C

Readers D

Readers E

The Glass Mountain

Readers A: Once upon a time, there was a castle made of pure gold. It stood at the top of a glass mountain.

Readers B: In front of the castle grew an apple tree. On the tree were golden apples. If you could pick an apple, you could go into the castle.

Readers C: An enchanted princess sat in the castle. She was so rich!

Readers D: She was so beautiful!

Readers E: She was also the prisoner of a mighty eagle. He kept her on the mountain.

Readers A: Many knights tried to climb the mountain to free her.

Readers B: No one was able to get more than halfway up the mountain. They would always fall back to the bottom.

Readers C: Day after day Princess Rachel sat at her window. Everyone could see her.

Readers D: No one could save her.

Readers E: Rachel had been in the castle seven years.

Readers A: Each day she waited for someone to save her.

Readers B: One day Rachel saw a knight in golden armor. He rode a spirited horse. He was riding up the mountain. She was sure he would get to the top.

Readers C: When he was halfway up, he turned his horse around. They went back down again without a slip.

Readers D: The next day the same knight rode up the mountain. Sparks of fire flew from the horse's hoofs. They were almost at the top.

Readers E: Suddenly a huge eagle flew by. It spread its mighty wings. It hit the horse in the eye.

Readers A: The horse reared up high. The knight and horse fell down the steep mountain. The princess was not set free.

Readers B: The next day the princess saw a boy coming her way. Pete wasn't riding a horse. She knew he couldn't save her.

Readers C: But Pete had a plan. He had seen men try to ride up the mountain. He saw them all fail. He knew he had to find a better way.

Readers D: Pete went to the forest. He caught a lynx. He took the lynx's sharp claws. He put them on his hands and feet.

Readers E: Then he began to climb up the glass mountain.

Readers A: It was a longer climb then he thought. Halfway up, the sun began to set.

From *More Readers Theatre for Beginning Readers* by Suzanne I. Barchers and Charla R. Pfeffinger. Westport, CT: Libraries Unlimited/Teacher Ideas Press. Copyright © 2006.

Readers B: His feet and hands were torn and bleeding. He could barely hold on.

Readers C: Pete strained his eyes to see the top of the mountain.

Readers D: Then he looked below him. There was a big hole. Pete knew he could not fall. He would never be seen again!

Readers E: The sky was almost pitch black by then. The only light came from a few stars.

Readers A: It was too dark to climb anymore. Pete clung to the sides of the glass mountain.

Readers B: Pete fell into a deep sleep. He did not fall. He had stuck his sharp claws into the mountain. But he wasn't safe.

Readers C: Each night the eagle looked for anyone trying to get up the mountain. It circled round and round.

Readers D: The eagle saw Pete. It swooped down. Pete woke up as the eagle flew at him.

Readers E: The eagle tried to dig its sharp claws into Pete. Pete grabbed the bird's two feet with his hands.

Readers A: The eagle was stunned. It flew into the air. It lifted Pete off the mountain.

Readers B: The eagle began to circle round the tower of the castle. It lifted Pete over the apple tree.

Readers C: Pete drew a small knife from his belt. He stabbed the eagle. The eagle screeched. It dropped Pete.

Readers D: The eagle flew off. Pete fell into the branches of the apple tree. He put some apples in his pocket. Then he climbed down the tree. He took the apples to the castle.

Readers E: Princess Rachel met Pete at the door. She knew she was finally free.

Readers A: Pete had saved the princess. But there was still a problem.

Readers B: Pete and Rachel were stranded on top of the glass mountain. If they left the mountain, they had to leave the treasure. Only the eagle could fly the treasure off the mountain.

Readers C: Now, Pete was smart enough to climb up the mountain. Don't you think he and Rachel can figure out how to get off the mountain?

Readers D *(to the audience):* What do all of you think?

Readers E *(to the audience):* Or did they? It's your turn to be a storyteller. Can you come up with some clever ways for Pete and Rachel to get down the mountain with their treasure?

From *More Readers Theatre for Beginning Readers* by Suzanne I. Barchers and Charla R. Pfeffinger.
Westport, CT: Libraries Unlimited/Teacher Ideas Press. Copyright © 2006.

Big Klaus and Little Klaus

Summary: Two Dutch men are in competition with each other. Big Klaus is already richer and bigger than the other man. However, through deceit, Little Klaus becomes wealthy. Big Klaus becomes extremely jealous and greedy, and he tries to kill Little Klaus, who in turn kills Big Klaus. Preread this script to determine whether you wish to deal with the violence portrayed in the tale. Discuss how such stories were used to remind listeners that being greedy is a negative characteristic.

Readability: 2.2

Staging: The narrators should stand on the left of the staging area. Place Big Klaus and Little Klaus in the center on stools. Have Big Klaus on a much taller stool. The other readers can be on chairs, or they can stand to the side.

Props: The backdrop can be a rural setting, with a river. The students can be wearing old-fashioned clothing, with Big Klaus in more elegant clothes.

Presentation: Voice inflection should follow the wording of the script. In some places. the dialogue says, "Audience." Prepare these lines on cue cards. Have Narrator Three, a nonspeaking role, rehearse the audience on these parts before beginning the play. During the play, Narrator Three should hold up the cue cards at the appropriate time and prompt the audience to say the lines.

Characters:

Narrator One

Narrator Two

Narrator Three (nonspeaking, cue cards)

Little Klaus

Big Klaus

Audience

Farmer's Wife

Farmer

Preacher

Innkeeper

Cattle Driver

Big Klaus and Little Klaus

Narrator One: Two farmers lived in a Dutch village. Both were called Klaus. One of them owned four horses. The other had only one horse. The man with four horses was called Big Klaus. The man with one horse was called Little Klaus.

Narrator Two: The two men were very different. Little Klaus always wanted to please Big Klaus. So he would lend his one horse to Big Klaus to plow his fields during the week. Big Klaus was not as kind. He would lend his four horses to Little Klaus only on Sundays. On those days, Little Klaus was very proud.

Narrator One: On Sundays, the people dressed in their best clothes to go to church. They passed Little Klaus's field on their way to church. When Little Klaus saw people coming by, he would crack his whip over the five horses. He would pretend all the horses were his.

Little Klaus: Let's go, my fine horses! Let's get this field plowed.

Narrator Two: Big Klaus heard him say this one Sunday.

Big Klaus: You mustn't call them your "fine horses." Only one horse is yours.

Little Klaus: True. But I feel so grand when I lead all five horses around my field.

Big Klaus: I don't care how you feel. Four of those are my horses are mine. You don't own five horses.

Little Klaus: It's not a big deal. I won't say that they belong to me any more.

Narrator One: But Little Klaus could not help himself. If someone came by, he would act like the horses were his.

Little Klaus: Let's go, my fine horses!

Big Klaus: You must stop that! If you call those five horses yours once more, I will give your horse a crack on the head. It will drop down dead on the spot!

Little Klaus: Oh, all right, Big Klaus. I won't call your horses mine again!

Narrator Two: You must know what is going to happen next. A group of people passed the field. They said good morning to Little Klaus. He forgot his promise. What did he say?

Audience/Narrator Three: Let's go, my fine horses!

Big Klaus: That's it! I have told you not to say that my horses are yours. This time you will pay!

Narrator One: He picked up an iron bar. Then he struck Little Klaus's horse on the head. The horse fell down and died on the spot.

Little Klaus: You have killed my only horse. How can I plow my fields? How can I make a living?

From *More Readers Theatre for Beginning Readers* by Suzanne I. Barchers and Charla R. Pfeffinger.
Westport, CT: Libraries Unlimited/Teacher Ideas Press. Copyright © 2006.

Big Klaus: That is not my problem. I warned you. Your pride got in the way. You should have listened to me.

Narrator Two: Little Klaus did not know what to do at first. Then he decided to sell the skin from his horse, just like a trapper would do. He started for town with the skin. It was a long way. He had to pass through a great dark forest.

Narrator One: While in the forest, an awful storm came up. He looked for a safe place. But he lost his way. It was getting late.

Little Klaus: I am afraid I am lost. But I see a large farmhouse. I see some light. Someone must be home. Maybe I can spend the night there.

Narrator Two: Little Klaus knocked at the door of the farmhouse. The wife opened the door.

Little Klaus: Could I please spend the night here? I was on my way to town and got lost. It is so late.

Farmer's Wife: No, you can't stay here. My husband is it not at home. I don't know you.

Little Klaus: May I sleep on the thatched roof of the outhouse?

Farmer's Wife: I don't care. Just watch out for the stork up there. That is her nest.

Narrator One: Little Klaus crept up into the roof of the outhouse. He saw the stork by the nest. He lay down for the night.

Narrator Two: Little Klaus could just see inside the farmhouse. He could see a large table in the room. It was set with wine, roast meat, and some fish. The farmer's wife sat at the table, talking with the preacher. The farmer was not there. Little Klaus looked at all the food.

Little Klaus: If only I could only get some of that food to eat. It is a huge feast, and I am so hungry! *If only I could get some of that food!*

Narrator One: Little Klaus watched the road. He saw the farmer coming home. Now the farmer was a very fine man. But he did not like the preacher. The farmer's wife knew he hated the preacher. But she liked the preacher. And she always gave him her best food.

Narrator Two: They heard the farmer walking up the road.

Farmer's Wife: Oh dear! My husband is home. Hide in the chest. I'll hide the food in the stove.

Narrator One: Little Klaus could not believe what he saw. All that fine food was going in the stove. And he was so hungry!

Little Klaus: Oh, dear! Oh, dear! All that good food going to waste.

Narrator Two: The farmer heard Little Klaus. He looked up at the roof of his outhouse.

Farmer: Who's there? Speak up!

Little Klaus: My name is Little Klaus. I lost my way going to town. Your wife said I could sleep on the roof of your outhouse.

Farmer: That is not a good place to sleep. Come with me into the house.

Narrator One: They went into the house.

Farmer: Wife, this man is staying in the house with us tonight. Now, get us some supper.

Farmer's Wife: Yes, dear, of course. I'll get you some food right away.

Narrator Two: The wife brought them both large plates of porridge. The farmer ate a lot. Little Klaus still had the horse skin with him. He laid it under that table. Without thinking, he stepped on his sack. The dry skin in the sack squeaked loudly.

Audience/Narrator Three: Squeak. Squeak. Squeak.

Little Klaus: Hush!

Farmer: Where is that noise coming from?

Little Klaus: I am so sorry. It is coming from my sack.

Farmer: What have you got in your sack?

Narrator One: Little Klaus wasted no time. He began to lie to the farmer and his wife.

Little Klaus: Oh, it is a wizard! He says we should not eat the porridge. He has filled the whole stove with roast meats and fish and cakes.

Farmer: Are you sure?

Little Klaus: Just look in the stove.

Narrator Two: The farmer opened the stove. He saw all the food his wife had hidden there.

Farmer: What a feast. Wife, put these dishes on the table. Throw out the porridge.

Narrator One: The wife could not argue with him. She put the food out at once. As they ate the food, Little Klaus stepped again on his sack.

Audience/Narrator Three: Squeak. Squeak. Squeak.

Farmer: What is the wizard saying now?

Little Klaus: He says there are three bottles of wine in the corner. They are behind the broom.

Farmer: Wife, go fetch the wine. Little Klaus, can your wizard make the bogeyman appear?

Little Klaus: Yes. He can do anything that I ask. Isn't that true, wizard?

Audience/Narrator Three: Squeak, squeak, squeak.

Little Klaus: He says Yes. But he says we don't want to see the bogeyman. He is too ugly.

Farmer: Oh! I'm not at all afraid of him. What does he look like?

From *More Readers Theatre for Beginning Readers* by Suzanne I. Barchers and Charla R. Pfeffinger. Westport, CT: Libraries Unlimited/Teacher Ideas Press. Copyright © 2006.

Audience/Narrator Three: Squeak, squeak, squeak.

Little Klaus: He said he looks like the preacher.

Farmer: I say! He must be really ugly! I can't bear to look at the preacher! Is the wizard sending him now?

Little Klaus: I will ask him.

Audience/Narrator Three: Squeak, squeak, squeak.

Farmer: What does he say?

Little Klaus: He says to open the chest in the corner. You'll find the bogeyman. Be careful to hold the lid so that he does not escape.

Farmer: Will you help me?

Little Klaus: Of course.

Narrator Two: Together, they opened the chest.

Farmer: Ugh! Yes, now I have surely seen the bogeyman. He looks just like the preacher. This is a most useful wizard. Will you sell him to me? I will pay you a full basket of money.

Little Klaus: No, I really can't. Just think how many things I can get from this wizard!

Farmer: But that is why I want him.

Little Klaus: Well, you have been very good to me. I will sell him to you.

Farmer: That is great. One more thing. When you leave you must take the chest with you. I won't keep it here with the bogeyman inside. And who knows how long it will stay in there.

Narrator One: Little Klaus gave the farmer his sack with the dry horse skin. He got a full basket of money in return. The farmer also gave him a cart to carry the chest. Little Klaus left with his money and the chest. The preacher was still sitting inside the chest.

Narrator Two: Now, there was a deep river on the other side of the woods. The water flowed so fast that it was hard to swim. There was a great new bridge over the river. Little Klaus stopped in the middle of the bridge. He spoke aloud.

Little Klaus: Now, what am I to do with this stupid chest? It is so heavy. I am so tried. I think it is best if I throw it in the river.

Narrator One: He took the chest with one hand and lifted it up a little.

Preacher: No, don't do that! Let me get out first!

Little Klaus: Oh, oh! The bogeyman is still in there! I must drown him. I'll just throw this chest into the water.

Preacher: Oh! No, no! I will pay you if you will let me go! Please!

Little Klaus: How much will you give me?

Preacher: As much as the farmer gave you. My life is surely worth as much as the life of a wizard.

Narrator Two: Little Klaus agreed. The preacher jumped out of the chest. He pushed it into the water. Then he went to his house. He came back with a basket of money. Little Klaus started back to his home. He was quite proud of himself.

Little Klaus: Well, I have done quite well. My dead horse has brought me a lot of money. It will make Big Klaus mad when he hears how rich I have become. But I won't tell him just yet! First I will tease him just a bit.

Narrator One: Soon Little Klaus was back home. He sent a boy to Big Klaus to borrow a basket from him.

Big Klaus: Now what can he want with a basket? I'll just smear some tar in the bottom. A little of whatever he puts in the basket will stick to the bottom. That way I will know what he is up to.

Narrator Two: A few days later, Big Klaus got his basket back. Three coins were sticking to the bottom of it. Big Klaus went to see Little Klaus.

Big Klaus: Why are there coins in the bottom of my basket? Where did you get so much money?

Little Klaus: Oh, I got that from my horses' skin. I sold it a few days ago.

Big Klaus: You must have gotten a good price for it.

Little Klaus: Oh, yes I did. In fact, I am quite rich now. I guess I should thank you for killing my horse.

Narrator One: Big Klaus thought he could get rich the same way. He ran home. Then he killed his four horses. He skinned them and went into the town to sell the skins.

Big Klaus: Skins! Skins! Who will buy my horse skins?

Narrator Two: All the shoemakers and tanners came running to ask him what he wanted for the horse skin. He told them he wanted a full basket of money for each skin. They asked him if he were mad and walked away.

Big Klaus: Skins! Skins! Who will buy skins?

Narrator One: No one would pay what he wanted. It was far too much. After a while, the people of the town got tired of him. They told him to go away. Big Klaus realized that Little Klaus must have tricked him. He was quite mad. He even said he would kill Little Klaus.

From *More Readers Theatre for Beginning Readers* by Suzanne I. Barchers and Charla R. Pfeffinger. Westport, CT: Libraries Unlimited/Teacher Ideas Press. Copyright © 2006.

Narrator Two: Meanwhile, Little Klaus's grandmother died. He was not very fond of her. But he was sorry that she had died. He took her body to his home. He laid her in his bed. Then he went into the kitchen. By this time, Big Klaus was back in town. He was ready to kill Little Klaus. He came to the house with his axe. He knew where Little Klaus's bed was. He went to the bed and saw someone in it. He thought it was Little Klaus. So he struck the bed with his axe. And he hit the grandmother on the head. He left a big hole in her head.

Big Klaus: There! Now you won't get the best of me again!

Narrator One: Big Klaus went home. He thought he had killed Little Klaus. He had no idea that Little Klaus had been watching him.

Little Klaus: What a wicked man he is! I can't believe he was going to kill me! It is a good thing that my grandmother was already dead. He would have killed her! I must think of something to do with her body. I can't let anyone here see her with this hole in her head. They might think I have killed her. I have an idea! I think I can get rid of her body.

Narrator Two: Little Klaus dressed his grandmother in her best clothes. He put her in the cart. He left the next day while it was still dark. By the time the sun rose, they were in front of a large inn. Little Klaus went in to get a drink. The innkeeper was very rich. But he had a bad temper. The innkeeper spoke with him.

Innkeeper: You are on the road early today.

Little Klaus: I am taking my grandmother home for a visit. She is sitting outside in the cart. I cannot bring her in. Could you take her a glass of milk?

Innkeeper: Of course I can.

Little Klaus: You will have to speak loud. She is very hard of hearing.

Innkeeper: Of course I can.

Narrator: He went outside to the cart. Then he began to speak very loudly.

Innkeeper: Your grandson asked me to bring you this glass of milk.

Narrator One: She did not say a word. She sat still. The innkeeper spoke more loudly this time.

Innkeeper: Don't you hear me? Here is a glass of milk from your grandson!

Narrator Two: He shouted the same thing again.

Audience/Narrator Three: Here is a glass of milk from your grandson!

Narrator One: She never moved or answered. The innkeeper got mad. He threw the glass at her. She fell back a bit into the cart. Little Klaus had been watching from a window in the inn. He saw his grandmother fall back into the cart. Then he came running to the innkeeper.

Little Klaus: You have killed my grandmother! Look! There is a great hole in her forehead!

From *More Readers Theatre for Beginning Readers* by Suzanne I. Barchers and Charla R. Pfeffinger. Westport, CT: Libraries Unlimited/Teacher Ideas Press. Copyright © 2006.

Innkeeper: What do you mean? I didn't hit her that hard!

Little Klaus: Just look! I am calling the sheriff.

Innkeeper: Dear Little Klaus! Please do not tell what I have done. I will give you a basket of money. And I will bury your grandmother.

Narrator Two: Little Klaus was a happy man. He got a lot of money. He also got rid of the body. Soon he was home. He sent a boy to Big Klaus to borrow his basket again.

Big Klaus: Little Klaus wants my basket? It can't be so. Didn't I kill him? I must see him myself!

Narrator One: Big Klaus went into Little Klaus' house. He saw more money on the bed.

Big Klaus: I thought you were dead! Where did you get all of this money?

Little Klaus: You killed my grandmother. You didn't kill me. I sold her and got a bushel of money for her.

Big Klaus: You sold your grandmother?

Little Klaus: Yes, to the druggist.

Big Klaus: And he gave you a basket of money! How fortunate you are. I wonder if I can get money for my grandmother.

Narrator Two: Big Klaus went home. Then he killed his grandmother. He took her body to town to sell to the grocer. Big Klaus was run out of town again.

Big Klaus: That is it! I have been tricked for the last time. I am going to get rid of Little Klaus once and for all.

Narrator One: Big Klaus got a big sack. The he went to Little Klaus's house. He was going to tie Little Klaus in the sack and drown him in the river.

Big Klaus: You have fooled me for the last time, Little Klaus! First I killed my horses. Then I killed my grandmother! It is all your fault. But you won't ever fool me again! Once you are in this sack, I am going to drown you!

Narrator Two: Big Klaus carried the sack a long way. Then he came to the river. Little Klaus was not light. On the way to the river, Big Klaus passed the church. He heard the organ playing. The people were singing. Big Klaus put down the sack by the door of the church to rest a bit.

Big Klaus: I think I shall go inside for a bit. Little Klaus cannot get out of the sack. I'll just be gone for a bit.

Narrator One: As soon as he went in the church, Little Klaus cried out.

Little Klaus: Oh, dear! Oh, dear! How am I going to get out of this sack?

Narrator Two: Just then an old cattle driver came by. He had long, white hair. He was driving a herd of cows. One of the cows pushed up against the sack. It turned over.

Little Klaus: Oh, no! Please, I am too young to die!

Cattle Driver: Who is in the sack?

Little Klaus: Please help me. Open the sack so I can get out.

Cattle Driver: What are you doing in the sack?

Little Klaus: Big Klaus tied me in it. He is going to take me to the river and drown me. But I don't want to die. I have too much to live for.

Cattle Driver: You are lucky. I am poor and very old. I long to die!

Little Klaus: Well, I can fix that. Get in the sack and I will tie you in. Then, when Big Klaus throws the sack in the river, you will die instead of me.

Cattle Driver: I will do that. But you must do something for me.

Little Klaus: What is that?

Cattle Driver: I want you to take care of my cattle.

Narrator One: Little Klaus helped the cattle driver get into the sack. Then he tied him in. Little Klaus left with the cattle. Later, Big Klaus came out of the church. He picked up the sack. It seemed lighter to him.

Big Klaus: How easy you are to carry now! That must be because I am rested.

Narrator Two: Soon they were at the river.

Big Klaus: Well, here we are at the river. Down you go! You won't fool me any more.

Narrator One: Big Klaus started on his way home. Soon he met Little Klaus, who was driving his cattle home.

Big Klaus: How can this be? Didn't I just throw you into the river to drown?

Little Klaus: Yes, you did.

Big Klaus: Than how did you get here? And where did you get that herd of cattle?

Little Klaus: These? Oh, they are sea cattle! It is the most amazing story. But first, let me thank you for throwing me in the river. If you hadn't, I would not be so rich.

Big Klaus: But what happened?

Little Klaus: At first I was so scared in that sack. I sank to the bottom of the river. But I did not get hurt. I landed on soft grass growing at the bottom of the river. Then the loveliest maid met me. She was dressed in white. She said she wanted to make my life better. So she gave me these cattle.

Big Klaus: That is quite a story!

Little Klaus: That's not all. She told me that there were more cattle down the river. All I had to do was follow the riverbed and I could have a second herd.

From *More Readers Theatre for Beginning Readers* by Suzanne I. Barchers and Charla R. Pfeffinger. Westport, CT: Libraries Unlimited/Teacher Ideas Press. Copyright © 2006.

Big Klaus: But why did you come up here to the road? I would have gone after that other herd.

Little Klaus: Well I knew that staying in the river was the long way around. I thought I would take a shortcut on the land. And here I am.

Big Klaus: Oh, you're a lucky fellow! I would like to get some cattle. Would you help me?

Little Klaus: I could. But I will have to throw you in the river. I am too small to carry someone as big as you. Bring the sack to the edge of the river. Get in and I'll throw you in the river.

Big Klaus: Hmm. I hope you are telling the truth about this. If I don't get any cattle, you will pay.

Little Klaus: You can't blame me if you don't get any cattle. It is the maid who must give you the herd of cattle. It is not up to me.

Narrator Two: The two men went to the river. Little Klaus's cattle were thirsty from the walk. They ran ahead as quickly as they could to drink.

Little Klaus: Look how they are running! They want to go to the bottom again! I must stop them.

Big Klaus: Yes. But help me first or I shall beat you! Put a stone in the bottom of the sack. I must be sure I reach the bottom.

Narrator One: Little Klaus put a big stone in the sack. Big Klaus climbed in. Little Klaus tied it tight. Then he pushed it in to the river. Plop! Big Klaus sank like lead to the bottom of the river.

Narrator Two: Little Klaus drove the herd of cattle home. Big Klaus didn't come back to bother Little Klaus. All that came out of the river were three big bubbles.

Audience/Narrator Three: Pop! Pop! Pop!

From *More Readers Theatre for Beginning Readers* by Suzanne I. Barchers and Charla R. Pfeffinger.
Westport, CT: Libraries Unlimited/Teacher Ideas Press. Copyright © 2006.

Lizzie and the Cats

Summary: When the countryside is over run by mice and rats, a group of cats help out the town. The people reward the cats by giving them a house to live in and plenty of money. They hire Lizzie to cook and clean, finding that she is as sweet as she is hardworking. When she returns home for a visit, Father Gatto rewards her with gold. Her jealous mother and sister conspire to get gold as well, nearly destroying Lizzie's future with the prince. Adapted from "The Colony of Cats," a tale of unknown origin.

Readability: 2.2

Staging: The readers should sit in a semicircle in the order in which they first read as they read their parts.

Props: None.

Presentation: Voice inflection should reflect the script. There are opportunities for the audience to participate by saying *meow, mrowr,* and *purr.* If this option is used, have the cats rehearse the parts with the audience, cueing them at the appropriate times.

Characters:

Narrator One

Narrator Two

Mother Jater

Lizzie

Tom Cat

Cats (Optional Audience)

Father Gatto

Kitten

Poppy

Prince

Lizzie and the Cats

Narrator One: Long ago, a group of cats lived in a fine house not far from town. These cats were rich. They were so rich they could afford to hire help.

Narrator Two: You may wonder how they got so rich. Well, mice and rats used to run the town. They ate all the grain and corn. The people in the town begged the cats to get rid of the rats. And they did.

Narrator One: So the people in the town gave them a house to live in. They promised that they would have plenty of money.

Narrator Two: Now, these cats were clever. They could even talk! But they needed help with cooking and cleaning. This is the story of one young woman who went to work for them.

Mother Jater: Lizzie, fix your sister's hair.

Lizzie: Yes, Mother.

Mother Jater: Lizzie, empty the ashes. Scrub the floor. Wash the windows.

Lizzie: Yes, Mother.

Mother Jater: Lizzie, fix the dinner.

Lizzie: It's ready, Mother.

Mother Jater: Then go to bed. Now.

Lizzie: May I have a bite to eat?

Mother Jater: You? Ha! You don't deserve to eat. Why don't you just go eat with the cats?

Lizzie: All right, I will! I am going to live with the cats! It has to be better than living here.

Mother Jater: Fine. Leave us. But don't bother to come back.

Narrator One: Lizzie did not wait one minute. She ran until she reached the cats' house.

Narrator Two: Just that morning, the head cat had argued with the cook. He had nearly scratched out her eyes. Lizzie knocked at the door, just as the cook walked out.

Tom Cat: Who are you? Why are you here?

Lizzie: I'm Lizzie. Could I work for you?

Tom Cat: Can you cook? Can you clean?

Lizzie: Let me cook your dinner. Then you can decide.

Narrator One: She wasn't sure what they ate. But she began to fix some food. As she worked, she hummed a song. Different cats appeared in the kitchen to look at her. One cat sat in front of her feet. Another sat on the back of her chair. They meowed softly among themselves.

From *More Readers Theatre for Beginning Readers* by Suzanne I. Barchers and Charla R. Pfeffinger.
Westport, CT: Libraries Unlimited/Teacher Ideas Press. Copyright © 2006.

Cats *(optional audience)*: Meow. Meow. Meow.

Narrator Two: Lizzie kept working. A third cat sat on the table beside her. Five or six others prowled about among the pots and pans. Cats were here and there! Cats were everywhere! Lizzie didn't mind.

Cats *(optional audience)*: Meow. Meow. Meow.

Lizzie: I can tell you're all hungry. Dinner will be ready in no time.

Cats *(optional audience)*: Meow. Meow. Meow.

Narrator One: Before long, Lizzie had the cats eating out of her hand. If you walked by the house you could hear all of them purring.

Cats *(optional audience)*: Purr. Purr. Purr.

Narrator Two: Tom Cat asked her to help with the kittens. She even learned how to take care of the cats when they got hurt or sick. The cats began to love her.

Narrator One: An old cat lived in a barn at the top of the hill. All the cats called him Father Gatto. One day he came to check up on them.

Father Gatto: Is this new maid taking good care of you?

Tom Cat: Oh, yes, Father Gatto. We have never had such good help!

Narrator Two: Each time the old cat would visit, he would ask the same question.

Father Gatto: Is this new maid taking good care of you?

Tom Cat: Oh, yes, Father Gatto. We have never had such good help!

Narrator One: After a while, the old cat saw that Lizzie looked sad.

Father Gatto: What is the matter, my child? Have any of the cats been unkind to you?

Lizzie: Oh, no! They are all very good to me. But I long for news from home. I miss my mother and sister. I wish to see them.

Father Gatto: Then you shall go home.

Lizzie: I don't know if they will want to see me. They were mean to me. And they were angry when I left.

Father Gatto: You won't know if you don't go back. Have a visit. Then you can decide if you want to stay there. First, I have something for you. It is a reward for your hard work. Follow me to the cellar. I always keep it locked.

Narrator Two: Lizzie could not believe what she saw. There were two big jars. One held oil. The other held something that shined like gold.

Lizzie: What is in those jars?

Father Gatto: Oil and gold. I can dip you in one of these jars. Which is your choice?

Narrator One: Father Gatto waited for her answer. Lizzie looked at the two jars for a long time. Then she spoke.

Lizzie: Dip me in the oil jar.

Father Gatto: No, no. You deserve to be dipped in the gold jar!

Narrator Two: Father Gatto picked her up in his strong paws. He put her into the jar of gold. Then he took her out. She shone from head to foot like the sun in the sky. Only her pink cheeks and long black hair kept their real color. She looked like she was made of pure gold.

Father Gatto: Go home and see your mother and sister. But be careful. If you hear a blackbird crowing, look at it. But if you hear a donkey bray, look the other way.

Narrator One: Lizzie was so happy. She didn't even ask him what he meant. She kissed his white paw and left for home. Just as she got near home she heard the blackbird crow. She remembered Father Gatto's words and looked at it.

Narrator Two: As she did, a beautiful gold star appeared on her forehead. A few minutes later, a donkey started to bray. Lizzie heard it, but she looked away.

Narrator One: Soon she was home. Her mother and sister saw her coming.

Mother Jater: What are you doing here?

Lizzie: I came back for a visit. Look! I have a gift for you!

Narrator One: Lizzie put her hand into her pocket. She pulled out some gold.

Poppy: Mother! Gold! We're rich!

Narrator Two: Lizzie gave them all her gold. For a few days, they were all happy. She kept only her golden clothes. Before long, Poppy wanted to have Lizzie's golden clothes. She wanted to have a gold star on her forehead.

Poppy: Mother, I want some of that gold. I am going to see what I can get from those cats.

Mother Jater: All right, dear. Maybe the cats haven't hired a new maid yet.

Narrator One: The cats had not yet hired a new maid. They were happy to meet Lizzie's sister. They thought she'd be like Lizzie. And they were happy to have her work for them—for a while. Then the trouble started.

Cats *(optional audience):* Mrowr! Mrowr! Mrowr!

Tom Cat: Stop this fussing! Stop it now! What is wrong?

Kitten: It's Poppy, Tom. She is not at all like Lizzie.

Cats *(optional audience):* Mrowr! Mrowr! Mrowr!

Tom Cat: Hush, be quiet! Not all maids are pretty.

Kitten: I wasn't talking about pretty. She isn't kind.

Tom Cat: How can you tell? She just got here.

Kitten: She kicks us away. She doesn't pet us. None of us kittens like her.

Tom Cat: Let's give her a chance.

Narrator Two: A few days later, Father Gatto stopped in. He talked with Tom Cat.

Father Gatto: How is the new maid doing?

Tom Cat: Not too good. She hit a young cat with a rolling pin.

Father Gatto: Why?

Tom Cat: He wanted to watch her cook.

Father Gatto: Maybe she's better at cleaning.

Tom Cat: Look around you. Dust is piled up in the corners. Spiderwebs are everywhere. She didn't make the beds today.

Father Gatto: Give it a few days. I'll check on you then.

Narrator One: Meanwhile, Lizzie was sewing at home. The king's son was taking a walk. He saw Lizzie through the window. He saw how beautiful she was. He kept walking back and forth by the house. Finally, he knocked on the door. Lizzie opened it to see the handsome prince. It was love at first sight for both of them. They spent a long time talking. Then the prince had to leave.

Prince: Lizzie, I must leave for now. I would like to come back for you. Will you marry me? I know we'll be happy.

Lizzie: I would like that.

Prince: I'll be back for you at the end of the week.

Narrator Two: Mother Jater was hiding behind the door. She heard everything. She could not believe that Lizzie would one day be queen.

Mother Jater: Lizzie, a queen? My Poppy should be queen, not her! I'll have to figure out a plan.

Narrator One: A few days later Father Gatto came by the cats' house. He found the house in an uproar.

Kitten: Father, Poppy kicked Aunt Whiskers with her big shoe. Her paw looks broken.

Tom Cat: She hit Uncle Pete with a chair! He has a huge sore in his back. And she shut the three littlest kittens up in the attic. They could have died of hunger.

Kitten: Please send her away, Father! Lizzie won't be angry with us if you do. She knows what her sister is like!

Father Gatto: Where is Poppy now?

Tom Cat: In the kitchen, I think. The door is closed, so it's hard to know.

Father Gatto: I'll go see. I'll take care of it.

Narrator Two: Father Gatto took Poppy to the cellar and showed her the two jars.

Father Gatto: In which of these shall I dip you?

Poppy: In the gold!

Father Gatto: You do not deserve it!

Narrator One: His voice sounded like thunder. He threw her into the jar of oil. It covered her mouth and nose. She couldn't breathe. She pulled herself to the top of the jar.

Poppy: Get me out!

Narrator Two: Father Gatto grabbed her and pulled her out. Then he rolled her in the ashes on the floor. She got up, dirty and angry. He threw her out the door.

Father Gatto: Get out of here and never come back. One last thing. When you meet a braying donkey, be sure to turn your head and look at him.

Narrator One: Poppy set off for home. She was almost at her mother's house when she heard the voice of a donkey loudly braying. Quickly she turned her head toward it. She felt something on her forehead. She reached up. There, stuck on her forehead, was a donkey's tail! She ran home, yelling with rage.

Mother Jater: Lizzie! Clean up your sister. And get that tail off her forehead!

Narrator Two: Lizzie worked and worked. But she couldn't get the tail off. She couldn't even cut it off.

Narrator One: Mother Jater was furious. She blamed Lizzie for the problems. First, she beat her with the broom. Then she took her to the well. She dropped her into it. She left her at the bottom of the well. Lizzie cried for help. Tom Cat was out for his evening prowl. He heard her cries.

Tom Cat: Lizzie, is that you?

Lizzie: Yes! My mother threw me in! Can you help me?

Tom Cat: Not by myself. But don't give up! I'll think of something.

Narrator Two: The next morning, Mother Jater remembered that the prince was coming back.

Mother Jater: Poppy! Get dressed. And come in here.

Poppy: No, Mother. I can't be seen like this!

Mother Jater: Stop fussing. I have a plan.

Narrator One: Mother Jater pinned the donkey tail around her head. She made it look like it was hair. Then she wrapped Poppy in a large white veil. When the prince arrived for Lizzie, Poppy and her mother met him.

Prince: I've come for Lizzie.

Mother: She's ready for you.

Prince: Why is she wrapped like that?

Mother: It is our way. We wrap our maidens in white. Then they are ready for marriage.

Narrator Two: The prince had never heard of this. But he was young and in love. Poppy sat by his side. They headed for the castle.

Narrator One: On the way, they passed the old house where the cats lived. The cats watched at the windows. They had heard that the prince was going to marry a beautiful maiden with a golden star on her forehead. They knew that this could only be their adored Lizzie. But they also knew that Lizzie was still at the bottom of the well. As the carriage slowly passed in front of the old house, the cats began to mew loudly.

Cats *(optional audience)***:** Mrowr! Mrowr! Mrowr!

Prince: What is all that noise?

Poppy: Just keep going, dear.

Cats *(optional audience)***:** Mrowr! Mrowr! Mrowr! Lift the veil!

Prince: Wait! I think those cats are talking to us.

Poppy: Talking cats? Don't be silly. Just keep going, dear.

Cats *(optional audience)***:** Mrowr! Mrowr! Mrowr! Lift the veil! Look in the well!

Prince: Wait! Stop! Those cats *are* talking. I heard them say to lift the veil. And to look in the well.

Narrator Two: The prince lifted Poppy's veil. He looked at her swollen face. He saw the tail on her head.

Prince: You are not Lizzie! I'm taking you back right now!

Narrator One: The prince drove back to the house. He found Mother Jater.

Prince: Where is Lizzie? Bring her now … or you die.

Narrator Two: The mother was very scared. She ran to the well. The prince pulled out Lizzie. She climbed into the carriage. They drove to the castle. The next day they were married. All the cats came to the wedding.

Narrator One: And Father Gatto gave her away.

Cats *(optional audience)***:** Purr. Purr. Purr.

From *More Readers Theatre for Beginning Readers* by Suzanne I. Barchers and Charla R. Pfeffinger.
Westport, CT: Libraries Unlimited/Teacher Ideas Press. Copyright © 2006.

The Monkey Prince

Summary: A kind and beautiful queen dies during childbirth, leaving the king with a son. The king eventually remarries, and his second queen also has a son. A jealous queen, she conspires with a fairy to have the first son changed into a monkey so that her son can inherit the throne. Overcome at losing his elder son, the king dies, and the jealous queen's son is crowned. However, their plot is overthrown, and the sons choose to rule together in peace.

Readability: 2.2

Staging: The narrators should be on either side of the stage. Have King Richard and Prince Alphonse sit on high stools. The queen could sit on a tall-backed chair. The remaining characters can stand.

Props: The stage can be decorated with royal props, such as a crown, throne, and the like. A backdrop could have a tree with a green monkey on a branch.

Presentation: The queen should sound disagreeable and angry. The fairy should sound conspiratorial. The remaining characters should have normal inflection that reflects the script.

Characters:

Narrator One

Narrator Two

Fairy

Queen

Sir Thomas

Prince Alphonse

King Richard

Servant One

Servant Two

Lady Marie

Anne

The Monkey Prince

Narrator One: Many years ago there lived a king. His first wife was beautiful and kind. She was loved by all. The king was very sad when she died giving birth to their son.

Narrator Two: Soon it was time to give the prince a name. The king chose a wise queen to be his son's godmother. She was called the Good Queen in her kingdom. She named the child Alphonse.

Narrator One: After a few years, the king married again. This new queen was not so kind. Still, the king loved her. After a few years, she gave the king a new child, Richard. The king felt blessed to have two fine sons.

Narrator Two: The new queen was not happy, however. She feared that Prince Alphonse would inherit the throne. She wanted the throne for her son. She became more and more angry. Finally, she sent for her old friend, the Fairy of the Mountain.

Fairy of the Mountain: My Queen, what is it you want of me?

Queen: I need your help. I want to get rid of Prince Alphonse. But his father must not know that I was part of it.

Fairy of the Mountain: I would like to help you. But there is nothing I can do.

Queen: Why is that?

Fairy of the Mountain: Someone with great power protects him.

Queen: Who can that be?

Fairy of the Mountain: The Good Queen. She is his godmother.

Queen: But she lives so far away.

Fairy of the Mountain: True. But she knows everything that goes on with the prince. And she knows you can be as wicked as she is good. When you married the king, she gave the prince a large ruby ring. She told him to wear it night and day. It protects him from all that is evil.

Queen: How can we ever undo that?

Fairy: There is only one way. The ruby ring keeps its power as long as the prince stays in his father's kingdom.

Queen: Well, it should be easy enough to get him to leave the kingdom.

Narrator One: The queen tried to get the prince to leave. She failed again and again. Then one day she got lucky. The king's sister had not seen the prince for many years. She asked that the prince come for a visit. Prince Alphonse was now fourteen years old. The king agreed to the visit.

Narrator Two: When Prince Alphones was a child, Sir Thomas and Lady Marie had cared for him. The prince spent all his time with them. They taught him how to read and write. He learned how to be a wise ruler.

Narrator One: They loved him as much as they loved their daughter, Anne. When the prince set off to see his aunt, Sir Thomas and Lady Marie went with him. They traveled for many days. One day, they crossed a desert. The sun burned down on them. They were no longer in the kingdom. The prince's ruby ring could no long protect him. The queen and her fairy put their plan into action.

Thomas: Look, there are some trees. Let's rest in the shade.

Prince Alphonse: I am so thirsty. Is there any water nearby?

Thomas: Yes, I can see a stream from here. Let me get you some.

Narrator Two: Thomas did not know that the fairy had put a potion into the stream. It was just for the prince. As soon as he drank the water, no one could see him. They all looked for him. No one knew that he had turned into a little, green monkey. The fairy appeared to them as a wise old woman.

Fairy: Poor, sad people. You will never find the prince. Return to your own country. Tell the king that the prince is gone. He will be among you. But you won't realize it.

Thomas: What do you mean? How can he be here without us realizing it?

Narrator One: But the fairy had vanished. Thomas and Marie looked and looked for the prince. They had to give up. They returned to their country and told the king the news. He became so sad that he fell ill and died. Richard was made the new king.

Narrator Two: The queen was thrilled to see the crown on her son's head. Now she could rule through her son. She was a harsh queen. No one liked her. Many people thought she had killed Prince Alphonse. But no one could prove it. And they loved her son.

Narrator One: The young king loved hunting. He often spent his days riding and shooting. One day, after a long morning's hunt, he stopped to rest.

King Richard: This is a fine place for my lunch.

Narrator Two: While eating, he looked up in a tree. There sat a bright green, little monkey.

King Richard: Come here, monkey. I won't hurt you. Here, have some of my food.

Narrator One: The monkey took the food from Richard's hand. Before long, the monkey came down from the tree. Richard took him on his knee. Delighted with the monkey, he took it home. He trusted no one else with its care. The whole court soon talked of nothing but the pretty green monkey.

Narrator Two: One morning, the little monkey left the palace and went into the village. He went through an open window at the home where Sir Thomas, Lady Marie, and Anne lived. They found him to be a fine pet. King Richard sent his servants to look for the monkey. Two servants found him. They tried to catch him But the monkey cried and cried. The servants returned to the king.

From *More Readers Theatre for Beginning Readers* by Suzanne I. Barchers and Charla R. Pfeffinger.
Westport, CT: Libraries Unlimited/Teacher Ideas Press. Copyright © 2006.

Servant 1: The monkey is very upset, and we can't catch him. Sir Thomas was wondering if the monkey could stay there for just a few days. Then they will bring it back.

King Richard: Why would they want it to stay there?

Servant 2: They have grown quite fond of it.

King Richard: Fine, fine. Let them keep the monkey for a few days.

Narrator One: Later that evening, Lady Marie and Anne sat by the fountain in the garden. The little monkey looked at Anne with such sad eyes. They were surprised when they saw big tears rolling down his cheeks.

Lady Marie: Anne, this is going to sound odd. But this monkey reminds me of Prince Alphonse. Remember what the fairy said? "He will be among you. But you won't realize it."

Anne: Oh, mother. I think you are just charmed by his tricks.

Narrator Two: The following night, Marie dreamed that she saw the Good Queen.

Good Queen: I know you still miss Prince Alphonse. Do as I tell you. Go into your garden. Lift up the little marble slab at the foot of the great oak tree. There you will find a crystal vase filled with a bright green liquid. Take it with you. Place the monkey into a bath filled with roses. Pour the green liquid over him.

Narrator One: Lady Marie woke up. She hurried to the garden. She found the crystal vase filled with a bright green liquid. Then she quickly woke her daughter.

Lady Marie: Anne, wake up!

Anne: What is it mother? What is wrong?

Lady Marie: I've had a dream.

Anne: What is it mother? What

Anne: You woke me up because of a dream?

Lady Marie: Listen. The Good Queen, Prince Alphonse's godmother, came to me in a dream and told me to go to the garden. She told me where to find a vase. Look! Here it is!

Anne: What are you to do with it?

Lady Marie: She said to fill a bath with roses and put the monkey in the bath. Then I have to pour the green liquid over him.

Anne: What will happen?

Lady Marie: She said the spell will be broken. Prince Alphonse will return to us.

Narrator Two: Quickly they prepared the bath. They put the monkey in. They poured the green liquid over the monkey. There stood Prince Alphonse!

From *More Readers Theatre for Beginning Readers* by Suzanne I. Barchers and Charla R. Pfeffinger. Westport, CT: Libraries Unlimited/Teacher Ideas Press. Copyright © 2006.

Lady Marie: Prince Alphonse! Tell us! What happened to you?

Prince Alphonse: The Fairy of the Mountain put a potion in the stream. It turned me into a little green monkey.

Lady Marie: We must tell everyone that you are here. You are the true king.

Narrator One: In the meantime, the Fairy of the Mountain came to see the queen.

Queen: What do you want now?

Fairy: That monkey your son likes so much?

Queen: What about it?

Fairy: It's Alphonse.

Queen: So? It's just a monkey! No monkey can take away the throne from my son.

Fairy: I'm afraid it can. The Good Queen has broken the spell.

Queen: I'll fix that.

Narrator Two: The queen called for her son.

Queen: Richard, I have been told that Sir Thomas and Lady Marie are claiming to have found Prince Alphonse. They want to take the throne from you. You must find him at once and put him to death.

King Richard: Mother, you must be wrong. Why would they try to do that?

Queen: Because they have never wanted you to be king.

King Richard: All right, Mother. Just to please you, I will go see them. But I am sure you are mistaken.

Narrator Two: That night, Richard set out for the home of Sir Thomas and Lady Marie. He took some soldiers with him. Sir Thomas had asked Prince Alphonse to stay in the back room. When he opened the door, he was surprised to see Richard and his men.

King Richard: I have been told that you are plotting against me. I have come to ask you if it is true.

Narrator One: Prince Alphonse heard them. He came out of the back room.

Prince Alphonse: It is I you should be talking with, Brother.

King Richard: Alphonse! Is it really you?

Prince Alphonse: Yes. See, I have the ruby ring the Good Queen gave me as a child.

King Richard: Why didn't you come to the palace?

Prince Alphonse: It was safer for me to stay here. Your mother will not be happy to see me.

King Richard: Well, I am! You must return to the palace. You are the true king.

Prince Alphonse: I will return to the throne only if you will share it with me.

Narrator One: The brothers returned to the royal palace together. King Richard gave Alphonse the crown. At that moment the ruby split with a loud noise. Richard's mother disappeared.

Narrator Two: The Fairy of the Mountain had lost all power over them as well. The brothers were free to rule the kingdom in peace.

Narrator One: Now there is only one question that remains.

Narrator Two: And what is that?

Narrator One: Who do you think married Anne and lived happily ever after?

The Soldiers and the Dragon

Summary: During a great war, three members of the king's army decide to run away. When they find themselves on the verge of starvation, a dragon comes to their rescue. However, the cost for their rescue is servitude for seven years. Their only way out is to answer a riddle. One of the soldiers befriends the dragon's grandmother and learns the answer to a riddle, freeing them from their obligation. Adapted from "The Dragon and His Grandmother" of unknown origin.

Readability: 2.3

Staging: From left to right, have the readers stand in the following order: Dragon, Herman, George, Walter, Old Woman, Grandmother, and Narrators. After the exchange with the dragon, the soldiers should move to the old woman. Walter should leave the others behind as he moves across the stage to Grandmother. For the final part, they should move back to the left by the dragon.

Props: None

Presentation: George is a pessimist. Herman is the planner and sure of himself. Walter becomes the hero of the story although he starts off frustrated with their situation. Voice inflection should follow the personalities of the men as indicated in the wording of the script.

Characters:

Narrator One

Narrator Two

Herman

George

Walter

Dragon

Old Woman

Grandmother

The Soldiers and the Dragon

Narrator One: There was once a great war being fought by the king's army. The king paid his men very little. The men were always hungry. Three of the soldiers decided to run away from the army.

Herman: I have had it with being in this army. I'm tired of being hungry. I'm leaving. Will you come with me, George?

George: If we are caught, we shall be hanged. How can we leave and not get caught?

Herman: Do you see that large cornfield there? If we hide in that, no one can find us. The army will not go there. And tomorrow they will be moving on. Once they are gone, we can leave the cornfield. We will be free.

George: I guess it's worth a try. Why don't you join us, Walter?

Walter: Well, I don't know that your plan will work. But I am ready to get away from the army. I'll come along.

Narrator Two: That night, the three men hid in the cornfield. But the next day the army did not leave. They stayed camped nearby. The three soldiers sat for two days and two nights in the corn. They grew very hungry. They were afraid to leave. They knew they'd be caught and put to death.

Walter: I should never have let you talk me into this. We can't get away. We are hungrier than ever.

George: Just be patient. I am sure we can find a way out of this.

Narrator One: While they were speaking, a fierce dragon flew through the air. It saw the men hiding below it. The dragon swooped down. The men in the army were glad that it stayed out in the field. They didn't realize it was talking with the three soldiers who had run away.

Dragon: What are you doing in this cornfield?

George: We got tired of being hungry. So we ran away from the king's army.

Herman: We hid out here. We expected the army to move on, but it didn't.

Walter: Now we are sure to die.

Dragon: Why is that?

George: Because we may starve to death. And if we are caught, we shall be hanged.

Dragon: I can help you.

Herman: What can you do?

Dragon: I can get you past the army. But if I do this for you, you must do something for me.

George: What is that?

From *More Readers Theatre for Beginning Readers* by Suzanne I. Barchers and Charla R. Pfeffinger.
Westport, CT: Libraries Unlimited/Teacher Ideas Press. Copyright © 2006.

Dragon: You will be free for seven years. Then you must become my servants for seven years.

Walter: I don't think we have any choice if we want to get out of here alive. We will take your offer.

Narrator Two: The dragon took them in his claws. He flew high onto the air and over the army. Then he set the men down, far away from the army. He gave each of the men a little stick.

Dragon: When you wave these sticks through the air, money will appear. You can have everything you want for the next seven years. But then you will become my servants. To seal the deal, sign in my book.

Narrator One: He set a book before them. Then he told them that there was one way out of the deal.

Dragon: There is one way to escape being my servants. At the end of your seven years of freedom, I will tell you a riddle. If you can answer my riddle, you shall be free.

Narrator Two: The dragon flew away. The three soldiers began their seven years of freedom. They had as much money as they wanted. They were never hungry. The years raced by. The three soldiers were still together.

George: The seven years are nearly over. I wonder when the dragon will come for us?

Herman: I wonder what will happen to us when he does come!

Walter: Don't worry. I bet I can guess the answer to the dragon's riddle. Then we shall be free.

George: I'm not so sure. He's a clever dragon. Perhaps we should try to find a way out of this.

Narrator One: The three of them sat down in an open field. They thought and thought. They looked so sad. An old woman passing by saw them. She stopped and talked with them.

Old Woman: Why do you look so sad?

George: Don't bother us, old woman. We are trying to solve a life-and-death problem. I doubt if you could help.

Old Woman: Who knows? Tell me. What is this problem?

Herman: A dragon saved us from the king's army. He said we could have seven years of freedom. Then we would become his servants for seven years.

Walter: He had us sign our names in his book. We've had seven years of wealth and freedom. Now we face seven years of servitude.

George: There is only one chance that we can get out of it.

Old Woman: What is that?

From *More Readers Theatre for Beginning Readers* by Suzanne I. Barchers and Charla R. Pfeffinger. Westport, CT: Libraries Unlimited/Teacher Ideas Press. Copyright © 2006.

Herman: We have to answer his riddle. He seems very clever. We fear we may never be free of him.

Old Woman: If you want to be free, you must help yourselves.

Walter: We would if we knew what to do.

Old Woman: I can tell you. One of you must go into the wood. There you will come upon a building of rocks. It looks like a little house that is tumbling down. Go inside. You will find help there. Good luck and goodbye.

Narrator Two: With those words, the old woman disappeared.

George: How does that save us?

Herman: It sounds like a wild goose chase to me.

Walter: Well, it won't hurt for one of us to go. Maybe she knows something we don't know. Maybe it's her way of telling us how to get the answer to the riddle.

George: Go if you want to. I am staying right here.

Herman: Me, too. Why don't you go, Walter? You seem to think she can help. And good luck to you. You'll need it out there in that wood.

Narrator One: So Walter went into the wood until he found the rock hut. In the hut sat a very old woman. He didn't know that she was the dragon's grandmother.

Grandmother: Why are you here, young man?

Walter: It's a long story.

Grandmother: I have nothing to do. Have a seat and tell me your story.

Narrator Two: Walter told her all that had happened. She liked Walter a great deal. She decided to help him.

Grandmother: Young man, I think I can help you. As it turns out, I'm this dragon's grandmother.

Walter: What? How can that be?

Grandmother: Never mind. Just do just as I say.

Walter: I will.

Narrator One: She lifted up a large stone that lay over the cellar door.

Grandmother: Hide yourself in here. Soon the dragon will come home for dinner. I will ask him about the riddle. You will be able to hear all we say. He tells me everything, so listen carefully.

Narrator Two: At midnight. the dragon flew in. He asked for his supper. His grandmother laid the table and brought out the food. While they ate, she asked the dragon about his day.

From *More Readers Theatre for Beginning Readers* by Suzanne I. Barchers and Charla R. Pfeffinger. Westport, CT: Libraries Unlimited/Teacher Ideas Press. Copyright © 2006.

Grandmother: What have you done today? How many men have you captured?

Dragon: I haven't had much luck today. But I do have three soldiers who will be mine soon.

Grandmother: Indeed! Three soldiers! And they cannot escape from you?

Dragon: They are mine as soon as their seven years of freedom are up. Then I shall give them one chance at freedom.

Grandmother: What will they have to do?

Dragon: They will have to answer a riddle.

Grandmother: What sort of a riddle?

Dragon: I will tell you how it goes. I'm going to ask them what I'll be serving them for their first meal. Their roast meat shall be a dead sea cat that lies in the North Sea. The rib of a whale shall be their silver spoon. The hollow hoof of a horse shall be their wineglass. They will never guess all three parts to the riddle.

Narrator One: When the dragon had gone to bed, his old grandmother pulled up the stone. She let Walter out of his hiding place.

Grandmother: Did you listen to what he said?

Walter: Yes, thank you. I think I can set us free.

Narrator Two: Walter found his friends still sitting in the field.

George: Where have you been?

Herman: We were worried about you.

Walter: There was no need to worry. I have the answer to the riddle.

George: How did that happen?

Walter: I met his grandmother. She tricked him into telling the answer to the riddle. I was hiding where I could hear it.

Herman: This is great! We may be free of the dragon after all. Tell us, what are the answers?

Narrator One: It wasn't long before the dragon arrived.

Dragon: I am going to take you with me to my home. Then I will ask you the riddle. If you can answer it, you will be free of me forever. I will even let you keep the magic sticks.

Narrator Two: When they arrived at the dragon's home, he asked the first part of the riddle.

Dragon: Can you tell me what you will get for your roast meat tonight for dinner?

George: A dead sea cat that lies in the North Sea.

Dragon: How could you know that? Just a lucky guess. Here is part two. What shall be your spoon?

Herman: Oh, I know. The rib of a whale shall be our silver spoon.

Dragon: Hmm, hmm, hmm. This is very strange. Well, let's see how clever you are, Walter. Do you know what your wineglass shall be?

Walter: The hollow hoof of a horse shall be our wineglass.

Dragon (*angrily*): How could you know those answers! I thought I was so clever. Now I have to let you go.

Narrator One: The dragon flew away with a loud shriek. It never returned. The three soldiers lived happily together. They were never hungry again.

From *More Readers Theatre for Beginning Readers* by Suzanne I. Barchers and Charla R. Pfeffinger. Westport, CT: Libraries Unlimited/Teacher Ideas Press. Copyright © 2006.

Boots and His Brothers

Summary: In this adapted tale from Norway, three brothers try to win the hand of a princess. They have to complete two tasks. One is to cut down an oak tree, and the other is to dig a well. As they travel to the palace, Boots, the youngest and most curious brother, finds three objects that help him complete the tasks. Ignoring his brothers, he follows his instincts and succeeds at both tasks.

Readability: 2.4

Staging: Narrators should be off to one side. The king and queen should be at the other side of the stage. The axe, spade, and walnut should be in the middle. The brothers can start by the narrators and walk in turn toward the axe, spade, and walnut. Remind them to keep facing forward when they speak.

Props: The brothers can dress in poor clothing. The king and queen can be dressed in royal clothes. The axe, spade, and walnut should be dressed simply.

Characters:

Narrator One

Narrator Two

King

Queen

Peter

Paul

Boots

Axe

Spade

Walnut

Boots and His Brothers

Narrator One: Once a poor widow had three sons. There names were Peter, Paul, and John. John was the youngest. He was called Boots because he always wore hand-me-down boots that were too big. They were very poor, so the boys went out to find their fortune.

Narrator Two: The king had an oak tree growing in front of a window of his palace.

King: That tree blocks the sun. I wish it were gone.

Queen: Dear, the gardener has tried to take it down. The trunk is too hard.

King: I know what to do. I will pay a great reward to anyone who can cut it down.

Narrator One: The king sent word out about the tree. Many men tried to cut it down. It just grew bigger and stronger.

Narrator Two: That wasn't the king's only problem. He needed a new well dug. His well often ran dry. Other wells in the kingdom gave plenty of water. The king thought he'd offer a reward for this job, too.

King: I need a new well dug. I will pay a reward of money and goods to anyone who can dig it for me.

Narrator One: Several men tried to dig a new well. Each one ran into rock after digging a few inches. This rock bed was too thick to get through. The king decided he needed a better reward.

King: If someone can cut down that oak tree and dig me a well, he can have half my kingdom. And he can marry my daughter!

Narrator Two: Everyone talked about the king's challenge. Who wouldn't want half the kingdom and a princess to marry? This princess was lovely, very bright, and very smart. But everyone who tried failed at the tasks.

King: My grounds are a mess. There are holes everywhere! And that tree keeps growing stronger and taller. I don't know what I'm going to do.

Narrator One: The three brothers heard about the king's challenge. They thought they'd try to fell the tree and dig the well. They hadn't gone far before they came to a wood. As they climbed the hill along the wood, they heard something chopping at the trees ahead of them.

Boots: I wonder who it is that is chopping those trees up there? I'd like to find out.

Peter: We need to get to the palace.

Paul: Why are you always so curious, Boots? Let's keep going.

Peter: You're right, Paul. We don't have time to stop.

Boots: I am going to go up and see what is going on.

From *More Readers Theatre for Beginning Readers* by Suzanne I. Barchers and Charla R. Pfeffinger.
Westport, CT: Libraries Unlimited/Teacher Ideas Press. Copyright © 2006.

Peter *(teasing):* If you're lucky maybe you can get a lesson in a woodcutting.

Narrator Two: Boots ignored his brother. Soon he reached the place where he heard the chopping. There he saw an axe chopping at the trunk of a tree all by itself. Boots spoke to the axe as if it were alive.

Boots: Good day! Do you stand here all day and chop?

Axe: Yes.

Boots: Why would you do that?

Axe: I have been waiting for you to come along.

Boots: Well, here I am at last. May I take you with me?

Axe: That's why I am here.

Narrator One: Boots took the axe apart. He put the pieces in his back pockets. He joined his brothers. They began to tease him.

Paul: What did you see on the hillside?

Boots: Oh, it was only an axe chopping. We had better be on our way.

Peter: An axe chopping? I don't think so.

Paul: Let's just keep going.

Narrator Two: After awhile they came to a steep rock. They heard digging sounds.

Boots: I wonder who is digging at that rock.

Peter: It must be something else. No one can dig on a rock.

Boots: I think it I'll just climb up and see what's there.

Paul: Boots, let's keep going. You've already wasted enough time.

Boots: I'll be quick. Just walk slowly ahead. I'll catch up.

Narrator One: Boots climbed the rock. His brothers waited for him, laughing and teasing. When he got near the top, he couldn't believe his eyes. There was a spade, digging away.

Boots: Good day! Do you stay here all day and dig?

Spade: Yes, that's what I've been doing. I've been waiting for you.

Boots: Well, here I am.

Spade: Then let's be on our way.

Narrator Two: Boots took apart the spade. He put the pieces in his pocket. Then he joined his brothers.

Paul: What was at the top of the rock?

Boots: Just a spade digging.

Paul: What are you talking about?

Peter: Never mind. Let's get going.

Narrator One: The brothers wondered what Boots was talking about. But they were in a hurry to get to the palace. A bit later, they came to a brook. They were thirsty after their long walk. They stopped to have a drink.

Boots: I wonder where all this water comes from?

Peter: Don't you ever stop wondering about things? Who cares where it comes from?

Paul: You should know that anyway. All water rises from a spring in the earth!

Boots: Still, I would like to see where the brook starts.

Paul: Another delay? We'll never get there.

Boots: Just wait. I'll be quick.

Narrator Two: Boots walked alongside the brook until it got smaller and smaller. Soon he came to the start of the brook. There was a big walnut. Water trickled out of that walnut!

Boots: Good day! A walnut with water trickling out? What is that all about?

Walnut: That's what I do. I have been waiting for you.

Boots: Well, here I am. Are you coming with me?

Walnut: That's the plan.

Narrator One: Boots took a lump of moss. He plugged up the hole in the walnut so the water wouldn't run out. Then he put the walnut into his shirt pocket. He ran down to his brothers.

Paul: Well, have you found out where the water comes from?

Boots: It was nothing special. The water runs out from a hole.

Narrator Two: His brothers made fun of him as they walked along. But Boots didn't mind a bit. Finally, they came to the king's palace. Many people had come to try their luck. All had failed. The king didn't think people were trying hard enough. He made a new decree.

King: Those who fail at digging the well and felling the tree will be sent to an island.

Narrator One: The two brothers weren't afraid of failure, so Peter tried first. He failed and was taken out to the island. Paul failed also and joined Peter on the island. Now it was Boots's turn.

King: Your brothers failed. Do you think you can succeed?

Boots: I'd like to try.

From *More Readers Theatre for Beginning Readers* by Suzanne I. Barchers and Charla R. Pfeffinger. Westport, CT: Libraries Unlimited/Teacher Ideas Press. Copyright © 2006.

King: Go ahead. I am sure it won't be long before you join your brothers.

Narrator Two: Boots took his axe out of his back pocket and put it back together. He put the axe at the base of the tree.

Boots: Axe. Chop away!

Narrator One: The axe quickly chopped down the tree. Next, Boots pulled out his spade. He fitted it to its handle.

Boots: Dig away, spade. We need a well hole dug below the rock.

Narrator Two: The spade dug until the earth and rock flew. When the well was big and deep, Boots took the walnut out of his shirt pocket. He put it in one corner of the well. The he pulled the plug of moss out of the hole.

Boots: Trickle and run, walnut.

Narrator One: Water trickled until it gushed out of the hole. In no time, the well was full.

Queen: What is your name, young man?

Boots: It is Boots, Your Highness.

King: You have done well. Let everyone know that you now have half my kingdom. You may also marry my daughter.

Boots: I would be happy to have half your kingdom. And I would like to get to know your daughter. Then we might think about marriage.

Narrator Two: Boots and the princess got along very well. One day they went to the island together. Imagine how surprised Peter and Paul were to see them. They gladly got into Boots's boat. They returned to the palace together.

Narrator One: And the next year, the brothers all danced at the royal wedding.

From *More Readers Theatre for Beginning Readers* by Suzanne I. Barchers and Charla R. Pfeffinger.
Westport, CT: Libraries Unlimited/Teacher Ideas Press. Copyright © 2006.

Martin and the Magic Ring

Summary: When Martin saves an enchanted princess, he is rewarded with a magical ring. The princess tells Martin the secret of the ring. When Martin is ready to marry, he uses the ring to win the princess. The princess is evil and tricks him into telling her the magic powers of the ring. She steals the ring and runs away. Left behind to die in a prison, Martin's only true friends, a cat and a dog, save Martin and his ring. This is an adaptation of "The Magic Ring" of unknown origin.

Readability: 2.8

Staging: This story works well when staged in scenes. All the readers should sit to the back of the staging area and move into place during narration and as Martin is walking before they are to speak. Scenes with Martin's mother and when Martin is in prison should take place in the center of the stage. The village scenes should be on his left, where he walks to buy the cat and dog and where King John will be. The scenes with Ashley, King Stephen, and the mice should be on the right of the staging area.

Props: None

Presentation: Because there will be a lot of movement if this is staged in scenes, readers need to remember where their audience is and project their voices. The readers for the mice should have higher-toned voices or be able to sound squeaky. The readers for the butcher and farmer should sound angry. Other voices should follow the varied voice inflections in their part.

Characters:

Narrator One	King Stephen
Narrator Two	King John
Martin	Martha
Butcher	Whiskers
Mother	Big Red
Farmer	King Mouse
Peasant	Tiny Mouse
Ashley	

Martin and the Magic Ring

Narrator One: Martin didn't seem to have any common sense. After his father died, he took one hundred dollars and went into town to buy supplies.

Narrator Two: When he reached the butcher's shop the place was in turmoil. He could hear loud, angry voices and a barking dog. The butcher had tied a stray dog to a post.

Martin: Hey there, butcher, why have you tied up that dog?

Butcher: He ate the meat I had sitting on the butcher's block.

Martin: He was probably hungry. Let me have him.

Butcher: I'll sell him for one hundred dollars.

Martin: A hundred dollars! Well, so be it. Here you are.

Narrator One: Martin named the dog Big Red. Martin went back home with the dog and no supplies.

Mother: Why is this dog following you?

Martin: I bought him.

Mother: You bought a dog! I sent you to town for supplies. Where are they?

Martin: I spent the money to save the dog.

Mother: We can't eat the dog! Tomorrow take our last one hundred dollars to town and buy supplies.

Narrator Two: While Martin was walking to town he saw a man pulling on a string. At the end of the string he was dragging a cat.

Martin: Stop! Where are you going with that poor cat?

Farmer: I am going to get rid of it.

Martin: What has that poor cat done to deserve such terrible treatment?

Farmer: It killed one of my geese.

Martin: Sell him to me.

Farmer: No.

Martin: I will give you one hundred dollars.

Narrator One: The farmer took the money and gave Martin the cat. Martin named the cat Whiskers and took it home.

Mother: Where are my supplies?

Martin: I brought this cat instead.

From *More Readers Theatre for Beginning Readers* by Suzanne I. Barchers and Charla R. Pfeffinger.
Westport, CT: Libraries Unlimited/Teacher Ideas Press. Copyright © 2006.

Mother: You used all of the money for a cat? You are useless. Take your dog and cat and go away.

Narrator Two: Martin had no choice but to leave. He called Big Red and Whiskers and they left. On the way to the village, he met a rich peasant.

Peasant: Where are you going?

Martin: I am going to the village get work.

Peasant: You can work for me. If you serve me well for a year, I will give you a great reward.

Narrator One: Martin agreed. For a year he worked hard for the peasant. At the end of the year, the peasant gave him the choice of two sacks as his reward.

Peasant: You may have whichever sack you want.

Narrator: Martin looked into the sacks. One was full of silver and the other of sand. He thought about them.

Martin: This must be a trick. I had better take the sand.

Narrator Two: Martin threw the sack of sand over his shoulder and he and his pets left. He walked for a long while. At last he reached a great forest. There was a fire in the forest. A lovely young girl was standing in the middle of the fire.

Ashley: Please use the sand that you have in that bag to put out the fire.

Martin: How do you know that I have sand in this bag?

Ashley: Because I am an enchanted princess. Please help me.

Narrator One: He emptied the sand on the flames, and the fire went out. At the same time, the lovely Ashley turned into a large snake. It wrapped itself around Martin's neck.

Martin: Why have you changed into a snake?

Ashley: To get your attention.

Martin: Well, you have done that! What do you want?

Ashley: I want you to go with me to my father's kingdom. I will tell him how you saved me. He will offer you gold and silver as a reward. I don't want you to take it.

Martin: Why not? I would be rich!

Ashley: I want you to ask him for the ring that he has on his little finger. It has magical powers.

Martin: And power is more important than gold and silver?

Ashley: Oh, yes. You will be better off with the ring.

Narrator Two: When Martin agreed, Ashley was once again a lovely girl. They walked until they came to a wide field. There stood a magnificent castle. Together they entered the castle and went to the king.

King Stephen: Ashley, where have you been?

Ashley: Father, I was captured by a band of thieves. They tried to burn me to death. Martin came along and saved my life.

King Stephen: Martin, thank you. For saving my daughter, you may have whatever you want. Do you want gold, silver, or precious stones?

Martin: I do not want any of those things.

King Stephen: Really? What is it that you want then?

Martin: I would like the ring on your little finger. Every time I look at it, I will think of you.

King Stephen: I will give it to you if you promise never to tell anyone it is a magic ring. If you do, you will have only bad luck.

Narrator One: Martin agreed and took the ring. After Ashley told him the ring's secret, Martin went back to his own home. After several years, he decided it was time to marry. The king of his village had a beautiful, young daughter.

Martin: Mother, go to King John and tell him I want to marry his daughter.

Mother: You want to marry the king's daughter? Why don't you marry one of the girls in the village?

Martin: I am going to marry the king's daughter.

Mother: Only a fool like you would think you could marry the king's daughter.

Martin: You will see I am no fool. Do not come back home without an answer.

Narrator Two: The old woman went to the palace. As she began to climb the steps leading to the royal chamber a courtier called to her.

Courtier: It is forbidden for someone like you to come up these stairs.

Narrator One: She ignored the man and continued the climb. Another courtier grabbed her by the arms to stop her. She yelled so loudly that the king came out to see what was the matter.

King John: Bring that woman here! What do you want?

Mother: My son wants to marry your daughter.

King John: Are you out of your mind?

Mother: Please listen to me. You have a lovely daughter who is old enough to marry. My son is a clever boy. He would make you a good son-in-law. There is nothing that he cannot do. He wants to marry your daughter.

King John: Can your son build a magnificent castle?

Mother: Of course he can.

King John: Can he do it in twenty-four hours?

Mother: In twenty-four hours?

King John: Yes. It must be opposite this window. The castles must be joined together by a bridge of pure crystal. On each side of the bridge trees with apples of gold and silver must grow.

Mother: Is that all?

King John: No, there should be birds of paradise among the branches. At the right of the bridge I want to see a church. It is to have five golden cupolas. This is where your son will marry my daughter.

Mother: You expect all of this to be done in twenty-four hours?

King John: If he fails, you will both to be dipped in tar and then in feathers. Then my army will run you out of my kingdom.

Mother: Is this your final word?

King John: That is my command!

Narrator Two: The poor old woman cried as she walked home. Martin was at the cottage door when she arrived.

Mother: You are a fool to think the king would let you marry his daughter.

Martin: What did he tell you, mother?

Narrator One: Martin's mother told him the king's command.

Mother: If you can't do as he said, we will be tarred and feathered! Then we will be run out of the village.

Martin: Mother, you have had an exhausting day. Why not go to bed? In the morning everything will be fine.

Narrator Two: Martin went outside and took off the magic ring. He tossed the ring from the palm of one hand into the other. Instantly, twelve men appeared. They asked what he wanted. He told them about the king's commands.

Narrator One: The next morning when the king awoke, he looked out of his window. To his amazement there was a castle and a bridge of pure crystal. On each side of the bridge there were trees with apples of gold and silver and birds of paradise. A church with five golden cupolas was standing on the right.

From *More Readers Theatre for Beginning Readers* by Suzanne I. Barchers and Charla R. Pfeffinger. Westport, CT: Libraries Unlimited/Teacher Ideas Press. Copyright © 2006.

Narrator Two: The king was upset. He had been sure he was going to tar and feather Martin and his mother. However, he had made a royal oath. Martin became a duke and married King John's daughter, Martha. Martin was very happy. Martha was very unhappy. She wanted to get rid of Martin. And she wanted the secret of his powers.

Narrator One: One night Martha gave him a drink with magic powders in it. Martin told Martha everything, and then he fell into a deep sleep.

Narrator Two: She took the ring from his finger. When she was outside, she threw it from the palm of one hand into the other. The twelve men appeared and asked her what she wanted.

Martha: By morning, I want this castle and everything you built to be gone. I want you to put a hut here. Put Martin in the hut. Then I want you to take me far away where no one will find me.

Narrator One: The following morning, when the King John looked out of his window everything had vanished! In its place was a hut. He sent for Martin.

King John: Where is the castle and where are the trees? Where is my daughter?

Martin: I don't know.

King John: Somehow you have deceived me. I am going to send you prison.

Narrator Two: While Martin sat in prison, his pets, Whiskers and Big Red, wandered about the hut.

Whiskers: We need to help Martin. The king is so mad he won't even give Martin anything to eat.

Big Red: Really? I would think chaining him in that prison would be punishment enough.

Whiskers: We must do something! Remember that he did save our lives.

Big Red: I have a plan. Let's go to town. When we find the baker walking down the road, you must rush at his legs. That will upset the tray of rolls he carries on his head. I will grab the rolls. We can take them to Martin.

Narrator One: Together they ran into the town. Soon they found the baker carrying his rolls. Big Red made a rush at his legs and the baker stumbled. The tray was upset and the rolls fell to the ground. Whiskers grabbed some rolls. He and Big Red hurried to the prison.

Whiskers: Are you alive, master?

Martin: Scarcely. I am almost starved to death. I thought I would die of hunger!

Whiskers: Never fear. Big Red and I will look after you.

Big Red: Here are some rolls. Don't eat them all at once. We are going to find your magic ring. It may take a long time.

From *More Readers Theatre for Beginning Readers* by Suzanne I. Barchers and Charla R. Pfeffinger.
Westport, CT: Libraries Unlimited/Teacher Ideas Press. Copyright © 2006.

Whiskers: You must make the rolls last till our return.

Narrator Two: Whiskers and Big Red set off to find Martha and the ring. They asked every cat and dog they met if they knew where she was. At last they found her.

Narrator One: When they reached the castle where she lived, Whiskers went to the cellar to hunt for mice and rats. She pounced on a very fat mouse that she thought would make a delightful dinner.

King Mouse: Please, don't eat me. I am king of the mice. I can help you if you will spare my life.

Whiskers: Can you get my master's magic ring from the evil princess?

King Mouse: I can do that. Please, just put me down. You can trust me.

Narrator Two: Whiskers put down the mouse. The mouse summoned all the mice in his kingdom together. You would not believe how many mice there were! There were small mice and big ones. Some were brown, and others were gray. They formed a circle round their king.

King Mouse: Dear and faithful subjects, whoever steals the magic ring from the princess shall be honored above all the other mice in the kingdom.

Tiny Mouse: I often creep about the princess's bedroom at night. I have noticed she wears a small ring on her finger all day. Then at night she keeps it in her mouth. I will steal it for you.

Narrator One: That night the tiny mouse crept onto Martha's bed. He gnawed a hole in the pillow and pulled out some feathers. He threw them under her nose. When she sneezed and coughed the ring fell out of her mouth.

Narrator Two: In a flash the tiny mouse grabbed the ring. He brought it to Whiskers. Whiskers and Big Red hurried back to the prison.

Whiskers: Martin, are you still alive?

Martin: Barely. I am dying of hunger. I have not eaten in three days!

Whiskers: Your worries are over, master. Big Red and I have brought you the ring!

Narrator One: Martin took the ring. He threw it from one hand into the other. Twelve men appeared and asked what he wanted.

Martin: Fetch me something to eat and drink. Then bring me some musicians. I want to hear some music.

Narrator Two: When the people heard music coming from the prison, they went to the king. King John sent a messenger to see what was happening. When he didn't return, the king sent a courier. He didn't return either. At last the king went to see what was happening. He couldn't believe his eyes. When he saw the musicians, he knew Martin had very special powers.

From *More Readers Theatre for Beginning Readers* by Suzanne I. Barchers and Charla R. Pfeffinger.
Westport, CT: Libraries Unlimited/Teacher Ideas Press. Copyright © 2006.

Martin: King and royal father, I have suffered a great deal because of you and your daughter.

King John: Martin, I am sorry. You must forgive me.

Martin: That is asking a lot, your majesty.

Narrator One: Martin turned his back to the king. He took the ring and threw it from palm to palm. The twelve men appeared.

Martin: Rebuild my castle. Join it to the king's castle with a crystal bridge. Do not forget the trees, the birds, or the church. And one more thing, bring back my wife.

Narrator Two: It was all done as he commanded. Martin and the king went to the castle. There Martha sat in fear and trembling.

King John: Thank you for bringing my daughter back. I am sure she has learned her lesson. Please forgive her, too.

Narrator One: Martin forgave his wife and the king. Big Red and Whiskers stayed by his side forever. Martin never let the ring out of his possession again.

Narrator Two: And Martha learned that having power could only make you happy if you used it for good. Of course Martin knew this all along. A wise snake had told him long before.

From *More Readers Theatre for Beginning Readers* by Suzanne I. Barchers and Charla R. Pfeffinger. Westport, CT: Libraries Unlimited/Teacher Ideas Press. Copyright © 2006.

The Steadfast Tin Soldier

Summary: This Hans Christian Andersen literary tale is about a tin soldier and his love for a dancer made of paper. Our hero, one of a set of tin soldiers made as a birthday gift, has only one leg. This brave soldier ends up falling out of a window, which sets him on an adventure. Eventually he ends up home, but his fate includes being thrown onto the hot coals of a stove, where he melts into the shape of a heart.

Readability: 2.8

Staging: Narrators should be on the left of the staging area with the readers sitting in the back of the area. They should move forward during narration when it is their turn to read.

Props: None

Presentation: Ned should sound like a little boy. The soldier should sound brave and strong. The evil elf and Rat should be loud and sneaky. Nick and Art should sound excited.

Characters:

Narrator One

Narrator Two

Narrator Three

Ned

Evil elf

Nanny

Tin soldier

Art

Nick

Rat

Fish

Cook

The Steadfast Tin Soldier

Narrator One: A toymaker loved to make tin soldiers. He was a clever toymaker. He made twenty-five tin soldiers from the same old tin spoon. Each soldier was just like the other, except for one. The toymaker had run out of tin. The last tin soldier had only had one leg.

Narrator Two: They were dressed in red and blue. They carried guns. They could only look ahead. The toymaker put them in a wooden box. They were a gift for a boy named Ned.

Ned: Look at this! Tin soldiers! This is the best gift! I think I will set them all up on the table.

Narrator Three: There were many toys on the table. One of them was a little castle.

Narrator One: A beautiful dancer stood in the doorway of the castle. She wore a fine dress. She had a blue ribbon on her arms. She stretched out both arms. She lifted up one leg behind her head. The tin soldier could not see the leg behind her head.

Tin Soldier: That dancer only has one leg. She is just like me! She'd be a perfect wife for me. But she lives in a castle. The only home I have is a box. That is no place for someone like her.

Narrator Two: Then night came. Almost all the tin soldiers were put in their box. The tin soldier stood on the table. Everyone went to sleep except for the toys. Did you know that they come alive at night? That is when they play. Some toys played leapfrog. Some played tag. Other toys just talked to each other.

Narrator Three: Only two toys did not move. The tin soldier and the little dancer stayed in their places. There was a small box on the table. When the clock struck twelve, the lid on the box popped off. Out came a tiny evil elf. He was there to cause trouble.

Evil Elf: Hello, tin soldier!

Narrator One: The tin soldier did not look at the evil elf.

Evil Elf: Why are you staring at that dancer? Have you have fallen in love with her? What a waste of time! She is too good for you.

Narrator Two: The tin soldier still did not look at him.

Evil Elf: Very well, don't listen. You will be sorry. Just you wait!

Narrator Three: Soon morning came. Ned put the one-legged tin soldier on the window-sill. All at once the window flew open. There was a big wind. The tin soldier fell to the ground! It was a terrible fall! He landed on his head. His leg stuck up in the air. His gun was stuck between two paving stones.

Narrator Three *(to the audience):* Do you think the evil elf caused the tin soldier to fall? Let's see what Ned does.

From *More Readers Theatre for Beginning Readers* by Suzanne I. Barchers and Charla R. Pfeffinger.
Westport, CT: Libraries Unlimited/Teacher Ideas Press. Copyright © 2006.

Ned: Nanny, quick! One of my tin soldiers has fallen out of the window. We need to go and find it.

Nanny: Let's go quickly. It is about to rain. Put your overcoat and boots on. [*pause*] I'm sorry, Ned. I can't find your soldier anywhere.

Tin Soldier: Here I am. I am over here. Please pick me up.

Narrator One: We know people can't hear toys talk. These people didn't find the tin soldier. It began to rain. Ned went inside with his nanny. The raindrops came faster and faster. It rained very hard. The tin soldier was whisked away in the water. He landed in a gutter.

Narrator Two: When the storm was over, two boys came along. They were playing with a boat made from a newspaper.

Art: Nick, look! Here is a tin soldier!

Nick: Won't he look swell sailing in our boat! I'll put him in it!

Art: Look at that boat go. This is fantastic!

Narrator Three: The paper boat tossed up and down. The tin soldier trembled in fear. But he was steady. He showed no emotion. He looked straight in front of him. He would remain steady and not cry. After all, a soldier never cries. The boat passed through a long tunnel. It was very dark.

Tin Soldier: I wonder where I am? Oh, dear! I know this is that evil elf's fault! He must have cast a spell on me.

Narrator One: Just then, a great big rat saw the tin soldier! He lived in the tunnel.

Rat: Soldier, do you have a passport? Show it to me now! You have to pay a toll.

Narrator Two: The tin soldier was quiet. He held his gun more firmly. The boat raced on. The rat swam behind it. Chips of wood and straw swirled around the boat. The rat called out to the wood and straw.

Rat: Hold him, hold him! He has not paid the toll to go through the tunnel! He has not shown his passport!

Narrator Three: The current became swifter and stronger. The tin soldier could see daylight as the tunnel ended. At the end of the tunnel, the boat went into a big canal.

Narrator One: The boat whirled around three or four times. It filled with water. It began to sink!

Narrator Two: The tin soldier stood up to his neck in water. The boat sank deeper and deeper. The paper grew softer and softer. The water was over his head. He thought about the pretty dancer. He knew he would never see her again. All of a sudden, he heard terrible sound.

Fish: Forward, forward, soldier bold! Death's before thee, grim and cold!

From *More Readers Theatre for Beginning Readers* by Suzanne I. Barchers and Charla R. Pfeffinger. Westport, CT: Libraries Unlimited/Teacher Ideas Press. Copyright © 2006.

Narrator Three: The paper boat fell apart. The soldier fell into the water. The fish swallowed him.

Tin Soldier: Oh, it is darker in here than it was in the tunnel. It smells, too!

Narrator One: The fish swam up and down. It began to make the most awful motions. Then the fish became quite still. It had been caught. It was taken to the market and sold to a cook. The cook took it home. She cut it open.

Cook: Why, look here. It's the little tin soldier! Nanny! Ned! Look what I have found in this fish.

Narrator Two: The cook carried the soldier into the dining room. Everyone was excited to see the tin soldier. They put him on the table.

Narrator Three: He saw all the same toys still on the table. At the end of the table was the dancer standing in front of the castle. He was glad to be home.

Narrator Two: The tin soldier looked at her. He was hoping she would remember him. But she did nothing. Then Ned did something awful. He picked up the tin soldier and threw him into the oven.

Tin Soldier: Oh, Ned! Why did you do that? That evil elf must have made Ned do this to me. I am going to melt lying on these hot coals.

Narrator Three: There was nothing he could do. A good soldier never runs away. He was ready to remain steadfast to the end. Suddenly a door opened. A draft caught the little dancer. She flew off the table. She landed in the oven right next to the tin soldier. She burst into flames … and that was the end of her!

Narrator One: The next morning, the maid took the ashes out of the oven. She found the tin soldier. He had melted into the shape of a heart. There was nothing left of the little dancer.

Narrator Two: So what is the morale of this story? [*pause*] Never give up. Be just like the tin soldier, steadfast and true. He had a brief life. Yet he had quite an adventure. He could have given up when things got tough. But he never did. He remained steadfast— to the very end.

From *More Readers Theatre for Beginning Readers* by Suzanne I. Barchers and Charla R. Pfeffinger.
Westport, CT: Libraries Unlimited/Teacher Ideas Press. Copyright © 2006.

The Young Man and His Cat

Summary: A young man is distressed when he learns his father has cheated the poor. He decides to follow the advice he gets in a dream and gives away half of his father's wealth. He throws the other half into the sea. He keeps six shillings that float to the top of the water. After his mother dies, he takes to the road. As he travels, he uses the six shillings to buy a cat. He decides to ask the king for advice or a job, and his cat rids the palace of rats. Arthur is given a choice of rewards, which the audience can discuss. Based on "The Cottager and His Cat," an Icelandic tale.

Readability: 2.8

Staging: The narrators should be on the left of the stage. The dream spinner should stand behind the narrators or off stage. The script can begin with Arthur speaking with his mother on the right. As Arthur leaves home, he can move to his left where he visits the old woman at her home. Then he can move to the far right where he visits the old man. He should return to the center to visit the king, who can be sitting on a stool or in a large chair.

Props: A chair or stool in each area of the stage for the readers. An optional small table can go in each area to represent a supper table. Students can sit at those tables, if preferred.

Presentation: The voice of the dream spinner should come from behind the narrators so it gives the illusion of a dream. The reader does not need to be visible. All other voice inflections should reflect the wording in the script.

Characters:

Narrator One

Narrator Two

Dream Spinner

Arthur

Mother

Old Woman

Old Man

King

The Young Man and His Cat

Narrator One: Once upon a time, there lived an old man. He lived with his wife and his son. They lived in a poor, old hut. The old man was actually very rich. He never spent a cent. The family would often go without food. He had gold, but he would not spend it.

Narrator Two: One day the old man got sick. Before long he was dead. The next night, his son had a strange dream.

Dream Spinner: Arthur, listen to me. Your father is dead. Your mother is very old. Soon, all that they own will belong to you. However, your father made half of his money by cheating others. He took it from the poor. You must give that half back. Throw the other half into the sea. But watch the sea closely. See if any of the money comes to the top. If it does, catch it and keep it. Catch even the smallest bit of paper.

Narrator One: For days, the dream troubled Arthur. He did not want to give away the money his father had left him. He knew what it was like to be cold and hungry. He was looking forward to a little comfort in his life.

Narrator Two: Still, Arthur was an honest man. He would never be able to enjoy money from someone who cheated. He spoke to his mother.

Arthur: Mother, several days ago I had this dream about Father. Is it true that he cheated people to make his money?

Mother: Yes, he did. I wish it weren't true.

Arthur: In my dream, I was told to give half of our money to the poor. Do you know who father cheated?

Mother: No, I don't. Are you really going to give away half of our money?

Arthur: I must, Mother. I can't enjoy our good life knowing father stole this money.

Mother: There are many poor people in the village. Any of them could use your help.

Arthur: I am going to help as many as I can.

Mother: What are you going to do with the rest of the money?

Arthur: In my dream, I was told to throw it into the sea.

Mother: Throw it away? But why?

Arthur: I don't know, Mother. But that is what I was told to do. And that is what I am going to do.

Narrator One: Arthur gave half of the money to the poorest villagers. Then he stood on a rock that jutted into the sea. He threw the rest of the money into the water. Soon it was out of sight except for a tiny scrap of paper. He reached down carefully and plucked it from the water. Six shillings were wrapped inside. This was all the money he had in the world.

Arthur: Well, I can't do much with six shillings. But it's better than nothing.

From *More Readers Theatre for Beginning Readers* by Suzanne I. Barchers and Charla R. Pfeffinger. Westport, CT: Libraries Unlimited/Teacher Ideas Press. Copyright © 2006.

Narrator Two: Arthur put the money in his coat pocket and went home. For the next few weeks, he and his mother worked in the garden. They ate the fruit and vegetables they raised.

Narrator One: Arthur's mother got very sick one day. In a week, she had died. Arthur was very sad. He decided he did not want to live in their house anymore. He wandered into the forest, not sure where he was going. Before long, he was hungry. He came upon a small hut and knocked at the door.

Old Woman: Hello. Who are you?

Arthur: My name is Arthur. I was just passing by. I haven't had anything to eat or drink for some time. Could spare me something to eat or perhaps some milk?

Old Woman: Won't you come in and join us? We were just sitting down to dinner.

Arthur: Thank you.

Narrator Two: Two women and three men were at the supper table. He sat down and began to eat. He also looked about him. An animal sat by the fire. He'd never seen such a creature before. It was small and gray. Its eyes were large and very bright. It seemed to be singing in an odd way.

Arthur: What is the name of that strange little creature?

Old Woman: Haven't you seen one before? It's a cat.

Arthur: I wish I could buy it. It could keep me company as I travel.

Old Woman: If you have six shillings, you can buy it.

Arthur: That is just what I have left. I would love to have it.

Old Woman: Why don't you stay the night? You can take the cat with you in the morning.

Narrator One: The next morning he put the cat inside of his coat. He walked all day. That evening, he and the cat came to a house. Arthur knocked at the door. An old man came to the door.

Old Man: Who is it?

Arthur: I am Arthur. I am traveling and was wondering if I could spend the night here. I don't have any money to pay you. I just need a place to rest.

Old Man: Come in. I can't let a young man like you stay outside all night. You are just in time for supper. Come and join us.

Narrator Two: He went into a room where two women and two men were sitting at the supper table. One of the women was the old man's wife. The other woman was his daughter. Arthur took the cat from his coat and placed it on a shelf. They had never seen a cat. They crowded around it, talking about it. The cat held out its paw to them. It then began to sing. The women were delighted. They fed the cat until it could not eat anymore.

Old Man: Where are you from, young man?

Arthur: I lived with my parents near the king's palace. My parents died this year. I had no reason to stay there. So I decided to travel.

Old Man: And this thing you call a cat. Where did it come from?

Arthur: I used the last of my money to buy it from a family I stayed with last night. It has been good company for me.

Old Man: What are you going to do next?

Arthur: I have no idea. I just know I couldn't stay home. I have no one left.

Old Man: What about a job?

Arthur: I don't have many skills.

Old Man: Why don't you go to the palace and ask the king to help you?

Arthur: Do you think I should?

Old Man: Of course. You should not just wander around in life. I am sure the king could give you some good advice. Maybe he has a job for you.

Arthur: That sounds like a good idea. I'll go first thing in the morning.

Narrator Two: Arthur went to the palace. He sent a message asking the king to see him. The king agreed.

Narrator One: The king was at dinner with his court when the young man entered. He waved Arthur forward. Arthur bowed to the king. Then he saw several little brown animals running across the floor. Some were even on the table. One snatched a piece of food from the king's own plate! When the king swatted it away, it tried to bite his hand.

Arthur: What sort of animals are these?

King: Rats. I can't get rid of them. They get into our food, our rooms, and our very beds!

Narrator Two: Just then, Arthur's cat leapt out of his coat. It landed on the table.

King: What is that?

Arthur: Oh, I am so sorry. That is my cat. I'll get him.

King: Wait! Look! He just killed one of the rats. The others are running away! This animal is magic. What did you say it was?

Arthur: A cat. I just bought it. I wanted something to keep me company.

King: This cat is just what I need! My dining room is free of rats. I must give you a reward!

Arthur: You are very kind.

King: Just a moment. You have to make a choice.

Arthur: What kind of choice?

King: You may be prime minister and help me reign now. You will have power and wealth.

Arthur: That sounds fine. But what is my other choice?

King: You can marry my daughter. When I die, you will be king. Choose carefully. I could live a long time. So, which shall it be?'

Narrator One *(to the audience):* And now, it is your turn. What would you choose?

From *More Readers Theatre for Beginning Readers* by Suzanne I. Barchers and Charla R. Pfeffinger. Westport, CT: Libraries Unlimited/Teacher Ideas Press. Copyright © 2006.

Index

Bear, The, 6

Bobino, 27

Big Klaus and Little Klaus, 84

Blockhead Hans, 74

Boots and His Brothers, 113

Cat and Mouse, Friends Forever, 31

Clever Maria, 61

Enchanted Prince, The, 66

Fish in the Tree and the Hare in the
 Stream, The, 16

Flower Queen's Daughter, The, 39

Frank and the Giant, 11

Glass Mountain, The, 81

Hazelnut Child, The, 70

King Frost, 53

Little Green Frog, The, 20

Lizzie and the Cats, 94

Lute Player, The, 57

Martin and the Magic Ring, 118

Monkey Prince, The, 101

Proud Apple Branch, The, 44

Steadfast Tin Soldier, The, 126

Soldiers and the Dragon, The, 107

Three Brothers, The, 48

Two Frogs, The, 3

Young Man and His Cat, The, 130

About the Authors

SUZANNE I. BARCHERS, Ed.D., has written fifty books, ranging from college textbooks to children's books. (See books and other readers theatre scripts at www.storycart.com.) Currently the Editor in Chief and Vice President of Leapfrog, she has served as a public school teacher, an affiliate faculty for the University of Colorado, Denver, an acquisitions editor for Teacher Ideas Press, and Managing Editor at Weekly Reader. She also serves on the PBS Kids Media Advisory Board and is a member of the board of directors for the Association of Educational Publishers (EdPress).

CHARLA R. PFEFFINGER received her bachelor of science degree in elementary education and her master's degree in reading from Illinois State University, Normal, Illinois. Mrs. Pfeffinger was an educator in Illinois for twenty-two years before retiring. She has been a contributing author to *Learning* magazine, Storycart® Press, and the author of *A Teen's Book of List, Holiday Readers Theatre* and *Character Counts! Promoting Character Education: Readers Theatre*.